Thinking Smart

Also by the Author

Marketing as Strategy: Understanding the CEO's Agenda for Driving Growth and Innovation

Global Marketing: 10 Selected Case Studies

Private Label Strategy: How to Meet the Store Brand Challenge

Value Merchants: Demonstrating and Documenting Superior Value in Business Markets

India's Global Powerhouses: How They Are Taking on the World

India Inside: The Emerging Innovation Challenge to the West

Brand Breakout: How Emerging Market Brands Will Go Global

Praise for *Thinking Smart*

One never doubts Nirmalya's ability to bring a unique perspective to marketing and business. But, beyond this, *Thinking Smart* also demonstrates keen insight on topics as diverse as art, investing, and parenting.

– Cyrus P. Mistry

Nirmalya is truly a master of many subjects: of course, marketing and strategy, but as much of Indian art, of staying equanimous in all situations, and in particular, of effortless time management. Clear thinking, quick witted and an accomplished researcher, his perspectives are always unique and thought provoking.

– Kumar Mangalam Birla, Chairman, Aditya Birla Group

Nirmalya looks at the modern business world through the eyes of a millennial. He offers up his particular philosophy as a deeply compassionate human being. It's this broad horizon that makes his insights so valuable. Truly inspiring.

– Rakesh Kapoor, Chief Executive, Reckitt Benckiser plc

Most academic marketers have not had business careers. Yes, some teach and advise different companies on marketing. But the real test is whether they can shape their writings and consulting to fit the narrow attention span of busy executives? As marketers, can they take into account the broader business concerns of operationalizing a decision, including raising funds, taxation and other financial aspects? Professor Kumar is a rare exception who has dived broadly and deeply into the literature of marketing and management, consulted and served on the boards of many companies, as well as having been responsible for strategy at one of the most impressive diversified business groups in the world. You can't help but benefit from Nirmalya's wisdom.

– Philip Kotler, S.C. Johnson & Son Distinguished Professor of International Marketing, Kellogg School of Management, Northwestern University

Nirmalya is one of the most brilliant and calmest people I know – so I'm looking forward to finding out how the hell he does it.

– Sathnam Sanghera, author of Boy with the Topknot & columnist for The Times *of London*

Thinking Smart

How to Master Work, Life and Everything In-between

Nirmalya Kumar

HARPER
BUSINESS

An Imprint of HarperCollins Publishers

First published in India in 2018 by Harper Business
An imprint of HarperCollins *Publishers*
A-75, Sector 57, Noida, Uttar Pradesh 201301, India
www.harpercollins.co.in

2 4 6 8 10 9 7 5 3 1

P-ISBN: 978-93-5277-656-6
E-ISBN: 978-93-5277-657-3

Typeset in 11.5/15 Chaparral Pro Regular at
Manipal Digital Systems, Manipal

Printed and bound at
Thomson Press (India) Ltd

To

The many wonderful people that I met while working for the
Tata group in Mumbai;
My colleagues with whom I served on the Group Executive
Council (GEC), each of whom had one quality I coveted:

CPM for his genuine sincerity and smarts
HB for his Machiavellian political skills
MK for his amazing social capital
MR for being a gentleman with integrity
NSR for his functional thought leadership;

And, all my friends in Mumbai for their love and support
It was great fun!

All that is gold does not glitter,
Not all those who wander are lost;
The old that is strong does not wither,
Deep roots are not reached by the frost.

—J.R.R. Tolkien, *The Fellowship of the Ring*

Contents

Preface

On entry into the Tata group, I was keenly aware that I had never been a manager and did not possess the well-honed skills of an executive that my colleagues with their vast experience in corporate life did. But then, Cyrus Mistry and I were clear that my role was not an operational one. I had been hired to head strategy at the group level and be a thoughtful partner to Cyrus.

It soon became apparent to me that the big difference between being an academic and an executive was depth of thought versus a bias for action. As an academic, one is trained to think in terms of concepts and the circumstances (what we in academic research call 'moderators') under which a potential action would be successful. The same strategy could be successful or unsuccessful depending on the associated conditions under which it was being implemented. Furthermore, as an academic, one reads more widely to include both the popular business press that many executives consume as well as the less accessible academic literature.

By nature, Cyrus was curious and thoughtful. During presentations and discussions of strategy with the Group

Executive Council (GEC) and our group company CEOs, he often remarked 'we need to apply our minds more' on the topic at hand. For him, this was about the moderating conditions under which any strategy would be successful. Given that the Tata group operated in so many different industries and countries, this depth of thought to the 'conditionals' was essential for success. Because of the variety of environments and constraints under which different companies manoeuvred, one could not simply pursue the same action in different Tata companies and expect similar results. As a result, I found a kindred spirit in him.

Whenever I read something particularly useful to the challenges we were facing, I shared it with my GEC colleagues. Cyrus would sometimes pass these on to other executives in the operating companies that he felt could benefit. Rather than send emails each time I read something, at some stage I decided to collate everything during the week and send one email on Saturday morning to my GEC colleagues. This way it could be read over the weekend when things were less hectic and there was more time for reflection. After a few iterations, Cyrus urged me to share these weekend reads more widely with the 800 top executives of the Tata group. I was hesitant to do so as I felt it might be perceived incorrectly. However, I added some of our group executives and CEOs with whom I interacted frequently and thought might be interested. Over time, as the word of this weekend read spread, others asked to be added to the email list. Some friends outside the Tata group also heard about it and the list quickly grew to a few hundred subscribers.

My small team at Tata was highly motivated and adopted the continuous improvement model that I espoused. My executive assistant, Shibashish Roy, and Jude Rodrigues, who helped me create presentations, took it on themselves to make my life easier.

Rather than having to keep responding to individual requests to be added to the list, they decided to set up a blog where anyone could sign up directly. This made the administration a lot easier.

Despite my scepticism that anyone would be interested, the blog soon had over 1,000 subscribers. They also created a LinkedIn profile for me and started posting the weekend blog every Monday morning. I am deeply grateful to them as well as to Maria Romero da Silva, an intern, for making the blog a reality and pushing me to seek a wider audience. This book is a consequence of our efforts. Taking advantage of this opportunity, let me also thank the two other members of my team, Mohit Sampat and Wilma Lobo, as well as two other Executive Assistants, Shailesh Chandra and Mahesh Dumbre, who worked briefly for me. All of them were fantastic in supporting me.

After I was fired in October 2016, given the academic calendar, I knew I would not be starting any new position until the summer of 2017. The question was how to use this intervening time gainfully. Without doubt, I had been privileged to have had a unique career that combined being an academic at leading business schools with having been an executive at the highest level in a global corporation. Thus, the twelve months before I started teaching were dedicated to reflecting on what I had learnt over the twenty-five years working across so many countries, in corporations and academia and in almost any industry one could think of.

This book, taking inspiration from my blog and combining it with my experience, attempts to capture my learnings on a variety of topics. The goal for all academics is to say something that is counter-intuitive and make every experience a teaching moment. In capturing my counter-intuitive learnings that could be shared with others, it soon became apparent that the book would end up being about more than simply managing marketing, or even managing business. These are my life lessons.

The book, my eighth, is unlike the previous ones in its conceptualization. Increasingly, I observe, people, especially the younger generation, consume media differently. They tend to read fewer books, just as they buy fewer music albums. Instead they seem to prefer bite-size consumption. In contrast to the usual practice where a book must be read from start to finish following an author-imposed sequence, this book can be customized by the reader. Start at any chapter, read in any sequence, and stop reading when you feel there is nothing more that interests you. The fifty-two chapters, organized loosely in eight sections with titles that are usually a question, are self-contained and can stand alone. If the question interests you, dive into the chapter. If not, skip it, and it does not take away from the rest of the book.

The title of a book is the publishers' prerogative. After reading the book, Krishan Chopra and Sachin Sharma of HarperCollins India proposed 'Thinking Smart'. While immodest, I accepted it after recalling that my colleague Madhu Kannan often introduced me to visitors, much to my consternation, as the smartest guy in Tata. As the chapter entitled 'Does IQ Matter?' will reveal, I have always scored below average in IQ tests. But, I assume that 'smart' is an outcome of not where you start with the resources that nature endowed. Instead, it is a manifestation of a life spent in the pursuit of knowledge and contemplation; a journey that will never be complete. In academics, we know that knowledge progresses through falsification. What was received wisdom yesterday is demonstrated as false today, through reasoning or empirical evidence, under certain circumstances. It is with this humility that I present *Thinking Smart: How to Master Work, Life and Everything In-between*.

Section 1

Managing Hiring and Firing

Hiring and firing people, especially the core team that one surrounds oneself with, is the most important task for a leader. It is in concert with this core team that strategy is formulated, operations are executed, the employees kept motivated as well as the organizational values developed and sustained.

My corporate career began with my surprise hiring as head of strategy for the Tata group, reporting directly to the newly recruited chairman, Cyrus P. Mistry. In my experience, leaders forming a new team deploy one of two approaches. Some leaders sketch out the capabilities they require and then ask for the best person to be identified internally or externally. This is how I was recruited at the Tata group despite never having met Cyrus Mistry previously in my life. Alternatively, other leaders prefer to populate their teams by recalling the best people they have previously worked with, and trust. Thus, for example, the new head of strategy at Tata under the current Tata chairman, N. Chandra, is someone who was previously his executive assistant about a decade ago.

Tata was universally viewed as the quintessential Indian corporate success story. Amazingly, around 675,000 people were directly employed by the group across the world. For any lifelong academic to be hired directly into such a prestigious and high-powered role was intriguing. I was a member of the Group Executive Council (GEC), the apex body of six individuals that included Cyrus Mistry, and we were charged with shaping the future of the Tata group. Given that Tata Sons had had only six chairmen in its, until then, 145-year history, it was commonly assumed that we were going to hand it over to the next generation when Cyrus retired.

No leader or hiring process is perfect. There will be mistakes in hiring that have to be rectified with firing. Consequently, in principle, I have nothing against the practice of letting people go. But, in fairness, one must follow a process. In the absence of fair process, even if the firing is a good decision, it will have a toxic effect on the rest of the organization as it makes the remaining employees uneasy and demotivated in the face of what seems like capricious decision making.

Before firing someone, it is essential to let the employee know that they are not performing using empirical data and/or behavioural evidence. Then, give them a reasonable time to improve with clear markers to track progress as well as support in the improvement effort. Finally, if, after a reasonable time, the necessary improvement is not observed, then the employee must be let go. This process ensures that the employee is not surprised at the firing, has had time to prepare for the post-exit and under the circumstances feels as fairly treated as possible by the organization.

The final conversation when the employee is informed of the firing decision should encompass three points. First, the employee must leave the room knowing they have been fired. All too often in the face of counter-arguments by the employee, the manager mistakenly leaves the impression that there is some wiggle room. But if the process above has been followed, then this is the final decision. Second, knowing that the first call the departing employee will make on leaving the room is to his/her 'sponsor' in the organization, the employee should be alerted that this 'sponsor' is aware of the current conversation. And, finally, reassure the departing employee that the human resources manager is waiting to help with the transition.

In my opinion, the firing of Cyrus Mistry wasn't reflective of an organization that prides itself for its values. The chapter describing it is a template for how not to fire someone.

My own tenure lasted for thirty-nine glorious months. Being fired for the first time in my life, with no advance warning, is a shock. If one changes the perspective from that of the organization to that of the individual being fired, then the importance of coping and bouncing back becomes paramount as we are dealing with a human being (and their family), no matter how flawed.

1

The Surprise Hiring

In January 2013, I was having a normal day in my office at London Business School when the phone rang. At the other end was someone from Korn Ferry. While I knew of Korn Ferry as a human resources consulting firm, this was my first interaction with them. The person queried whether, in confidence, I would like to explore the position of head of strategy reporting to the chairman of a Fortune 100 company that for the moment wished to remain anonymous. Over the brief phone call, it became clear that the position would be based in India.

During my academic career, I had been approached several times about permanent positions in the corporate world. For example, in the late 1990s, Deloitte asked if I would consider being the global CMO, a new role they wanted to create, and L'Oréal had an interesting offer for a marketing role in Paris. My standard response was always to say no and nip the conversation in the bud.

All I ever wanted to be was a teacher. Being an academic was central to my identity. And, in any case, through the various board positions, consulting assignments and executive education, I had more than my share of interacting with the business world. Consequently, I am not exactly sure what led me to agree to meet the Korn Ferry partner, as one's motivations are not always apparent to oneself. I know that I was a bit bored at London Business School and tired of the leadership that ran it.

After a decade at the school, I was on autopilot. My teaching, which comprised delivering four sections of the elective Advanced Marketing Strategy course every year, could be completed in twenty calendar days. No preparation was needed as I taught my own cases and books. What kept me excited was my research. Over the ten years I was at London Business School, I had written seven books as well as many cases and articles. All of this had led to substantial external recognition. I was fortunate to be frequently included on lists of top business school professors and management gurus in the world. The point is that I was at a stage in my career where after twenty-plus years I had achieved any academic goal I had ever dreamed of.

Undoubtedly, being in India intrigued me. Since 1995, I had been steadily moving closer to India in my research and consulting. Two of my last three books, *India's Global Powerhouses* and *India Inside,* were on India, while the other, *Brand Breakout*, was more broadly on emerging markets. Most of the board positions I held were with Indian companies. Between the board meetings and my research, visiting India ten to twelve times a year was not unusual.

The initial meeting with the Korn Ferry partner responsible, Peter Everett, was in Bangkok, where our travel schedules synchronized. Peter informed me that after a worldwide search they had settled on me as head of strategy and advisor to Cyrus Mistry, the new chairman of the 100-billion-dollar Tata group. Having conducted several interviews with executives from Tata for my previous books, I was quite familiar with the group, but had never run into Cyrus Mistry. We agreed to schedule a video conference with him on my return to London.

On further reflection, I realized taking the position would mean giving up tenure at London Business School, something that would be hard to reinstate if things did not work out at Tata. I decided that a safer strategy was to instead propose a hundred consulting days a year as that would allow me to keep my academic appointment. On the video call, Cyrus immediately dismissed the idea. He needed a full-time person based in Mumbai. I figured this was the end of it.

Korn Ferry did not give up that easily. Further emails led to a meeting being set up when Cyrus was next in London. Knowing that I could request a year off from London Business School without losing my tenure, I proposed to Cyrus that I join for a year to see if this would work.

My thinking was clear. First, I was not sure I would fit within a corporate environment or enjoy it. It also seemed that to succeed at this job, one needed close interaction with Cyrus. Would we be able to establish a relationship based on trust and mutual respect? From experience, I knew I do not suffer fools, even if they happen to be my bosses. Furthermore, I had been out of India for thirty years and uncertain if I would be able adjust to living there again. Finally, there was the question of compensation. What was on the table was lower than my LBS salary combined with my consulting practice. A year would be long enough to assess whether the excitement of the job and the amazing potential for an academic to learn from practice were worth the trade-offs.

I joined in August 2013 and stayed on. Cyrus and I were in a relatively short time able to establish an excellent working relationship. He gave me the space to work independently. More unusual in an Indian business setting was that he allowed me to disagree. He enjoyed that those around him pushed him to think harder and had some edge to their personality. On my part, I accepted his authority as chairman and that after expressing my disagreement, the decision was his to make.

After a couple of months, he kept inquiring periodically if I was ready to make a permanent commitment. Around January 2014, we had a meeting where I said I would stay and relinquish my tenure at the London Business School. In return, Cyrus said that while he could not immediately match my compensation, over the next three years he would get close. Since money was never a prime motivator for me, this was not a deal-breaker.

At first sight, the job of being strategy head for the Tata group may seem rather different from my academic role. But, it did not require much of an adjustment for two reasons. First, I was not the typical academic. For twenty years, as an external consultant, I had been working with top executives and helping them think through their strategy. This had taken me to around sixty countries working for over fifty Fortune 500 companies as well as many other smaller firms. The only difference was that now all my thought partnership was going to be with one group.

Secondly, my job was not to be responsible for execution. In fact, that is why Cyrus had asked the head hunter to explicitly consider only academics rather than ex-consultants or former corporate executives. An academic, he believed, was less likely to be tempted to interfere with the strategy or the running of independent Tata companies. The latter was the responsibility of the CEOs and the boards of the individual companies. Good corporate governance required us at the Group Centre to ensure that minority rights were not being trampled in any oversight that we had as promoters.

In our strategy discussions, we though hard about what the role of the group centre should be when our stakes in the operating companies was often less than 50 per cent. We finally concluded that in any diversified conglomerate such as Tata, the group centre can add value in essentially three ways:

1. *Optimizing the portfolio* by deciding which companies to fund, which to exit and which new areas to enter. This was the most important aspect of my role. Supporting Cyrus, and through him the Tata Sons board, on the portfolio decisions to be made over the coming decade was where the greatest value creation potential lay.

2. *Orchestrating greater synergies* between the companies provided the initiatives would be a win-win for all companies since the minority shareholders of the different companies were not identical. While one could spend considerable energy on this at the group centre, the relative upside was limited compared to the effort required. Rather than convincing all companies of the need to participate, the approach we adopted was to go with a coalition of the willing. With success, other companies would join the initiative over time.

3. *Nurturing the companies* was essential as it was how value was added to existing companies on a regular basis. This is what allowed group companies to use the Tata brand as well as access various stakeholders and enter new countries using group resources. Beyond this, because they were part of the Tata group, a company could access assistance from the group centre experts, myself included. Here I adopted a policy of providing advice to group companies only under one of three scenarios: I was on the board of the company as the Tata Sons

representative, the CEO requested me to come and help, or if Cyrus asked me to go and see what was happening with the individual company.

Of the three value-creation opportunities above, the first was where most of the energies went. To make portfolio choices required developing a strategy for the Tata group and Tata Sons in concert with the board of Tata Sons. Cyrus and I spent countless hours developing this strategy, taking feedback from the board, and then revising it. We had adopted a ten-year horizon with explicit goals for 2025 on what the group should look like. Once the board of Tata Sons bought into that, we could examine different paths that would get us there and allow us to pursue a long-term stakeholder value-creation approach consistent with Tata values and ethos.

This strategy was what we were pursuing when, suddenly, four years into his tenure, Cyrus Mistry was fired.

2

How Not to Fire an Employee

If you had an option of waiting five months to fire a CEO and avoid a loss of thirteen billion dollars in market cap for your company, would you take it? In any case, the last formal performance evaluation of the employee only three months ago was a glowing one. All you have are some differences on a few of the many initiatives he is undertaking to turn around the organization. In addition, perhaps, there is some personal animosity. But is that worth a public relations crisis that results in a loss for the shareholders of $13 billion in the next two weeks? Here is how not to fire an employee.

On 24 October 2016, Cyrus was in his fourth-floor office in Bombay House examining what seemed like a routine agenda for the Tata Sons board meeting that was scheduled to start in five minutes at 14:00 hours. Through the grapevine, Cyrus had heard that some of the board members had an unscheduled informal meeting earlier that morning. However, what they had discussed was unknown and, as such, he did not give it much further thought. The previous week had been business as usual with trips to China and Singapore to meet partners and investors.

A knock on the door, and to his surprise, enter his predecessor, Ratan Tata and Tata Sons board member Nitin Nohria. Cyrus welcomes them and asks them to take the two chairs opposite him. Nitin Nohria begins by proclaiming 'Cyrus, as you know, the relationship between you and Ratan Tata has not been working.' Therefore, Nohria continues, Tata Trusts have decided to move a board resolution removing Cyrus as chairman of Tata Sons. Cyrus is offered the option of resigning or facing the resolution for his removal at the upcoming board meeting. Ratan Tata chimes in at this stage to say he is sorry that things have reached this stage.

Cyrus Mistry calmly responds: Gentlemen you are free to take it up at the board meeting and I will do what I have to do. Nitin Nohria and Ratan Tata exit the room and walk over to the other end of the hallowed fourth floor of Bombay House, where the board room is located. Cyrus sends a text, 'I am being sacked,' to his wife Rohiqa before putting on his jacket and heading to the board room.

The Board Meeting

Cyrus takes his place on the chairman's seat, a chair that is slightly elevated and larger compared to the other chairs in the room. Mistry welcomes Ratan Tata (who has never attended a board meeting since Cyrus became chairman) to the meeting and informs the board that Ratan Tata and Nitin Nohria have something to share prior to considering the previously circulated agenda.

Nohria, a Tata Trust nominee and Dean of Harvard Business School, advises the board that the Tata Trusts have asked its nominees to propose a motion to the board of Tata Sons. Amit Chandra, another Tata Trust nominee, apprises the board that at a meeting of the Trust Directors held earlier in the day it was agreed to move a motion to request Mistry to step down as executive chairman of Tata Sons because the Trusts had lost confidence in him for a variety of reasons. No rationale for the decision beyond this declaration is shared.

In response, Cyrus argues that the articles of association require a fifteen-day notice before taking up such an item for the consideration of the board, and, as such, the present action is illegal. Amit Chandra informs the board that the legal opinion obtained by the Trusts stated such a notice was not necessary. He offers to share the opinion, but none has been to date. Instead, he proposes Vijay Singh to be elected as the chair for the remainder of the board meeting. Despite repeated protests by Cyrus on the illegality of events, Venu Srinivasan seconds the proposal. Ishaat Hussain and Farida Khambata say they would abstain on this motion to replace Mistry with Singh as chair of the meeting.

Quickly, a vote is taken with six members (Ajay Piramal, Amit Chandra, Nitin Nohria, Ronen Sen, Venu Srinivasan, Vijay Singh) voting for, while Farida Khambata and Ishaat Hussain abstain. Vijay Singh is installed as chair for the meeting.

Venu Srinivasan then proposes the inclusion of additional matters on the agenda by moving the Resolution below, which is seconded by Ronen Sen:

RESOLVED THAT the consent of the board be and is hereby accorded, to consider and resolve upon, in this meeting of the board, the following matters which were not included in the Agenda circulated for this meeting of the board:

a. Replacement of Mr Cyrus P. Mistry as the Chairman of the board and from each committee of the board;

b. While the board has adopted and put in place certain age criteria for retirement of Directors of the Company, to approve the cessation of application of the age criteria for retirement of Directors in relation to the Company;

c. Re-constitution of the Nomination and Remuneration Committee to consist of the following Directors: (i) Mr Ronen Sen (Independent Director); (ii) Mr Ajay Piramal (Independent Director); (iii) Mrs Farida Khambata (Independent Director); (iv) Mr Vijay Singh; and (v) Mr Venu Srinivasan;

d. Appointment of Mr Ratan N. Tata as Additional Director;

e. Election of Mr Ratan N. Tata as Interim Chairman of the board until selection and appointment of a new Chairman of the board in terms of the Companies Act, 2013 and the Articles of Association of the Company;

f. To take appropriate steps in terms of the Companies Act, 2013, and the Articles of Association of the Company to appoint a new Chairman, including by formation of a Selection Committee comprising of: (i) Mr Ratan N. Tata (Nominee of Tata Trusts); (ii) Mr Amit Chandra (Nominee of Tata Trusts); (iii) Mr Venu Srinivasan (Nominee of Tata Trusts); (iv) Mr Ronen Sen (Independent Director); and (v) Lord Kumar Bhattacharyya (Independent Outside Person); and

g. Until selection and appointment of a new Chairman of the board in terms of the Companies Act, 2013, and the Articles of Association of the Company, to vest substantial powers of management of the Company with Mr F.N. Subedar, Chief

Operating Officer, and/or one or more senior officials and/or Directors of the Company, subject to the overall supervision and direction of the board, in such manner as the board may decide from time to time.

Each of these resolutions is voted on in turn. While different board members propose and second the individual resolutions, the voting pattern is identical across them. Khambata abstains on each, Mistry objects to each as being illegal, while the others vote for them. It is all over in minutes, no explanations and no opportunity for Cyrus Mistry to prepare a rebuttal.

The Aftermath

By 3.00 p.m., Cyrus had returned to his office and begun packing his personal effects. He queried Subedar on whether he needed to return the next day. Subedar checked with Ratan Tata and reported that it was unnecessary. Cyrus then called his childhood friend and top-notch lawyer, Apurva Diwanji, to help him. Apurva arrived within ten minutes and asked for the Tata Sons' articles of association. Apurva realized that the press would inevitably be gathering outside Bombay House making an exit challenging.

Apurva needed a safe place for Cyrus to be taken as the press would be lying in wait outside the Mistry residence. Jai Mavani from Shapoorji Pallonji, the family firm of Cyrus, was given a call to organize this. Jai knew that Forbes, another Shapoorji Pallonji-related company, had its headquarters in the neighbourhood on a quiet street. Apurva exited via the side entrance of Bombay House, which was rarely used, to whisk Cyrus to the designated safe place.

The conference room is where Cyrus first got a chance to sit down, visibly shaken, and asked for a cup of tea. They knew they needed a public relations agency and a lawyer immediately. What they did not know was that Tata had already engaged six major public relations companies and booked many of the most prominent lawyers in the country in a bid to squeeze the resources available to Cyrus post firing.

At 5.00 p.m., Tata Sons released the following press statement:

> Mumbai: Tata Sons today announced that its board has replaced Mr Cyrus P. Mistry as Chairman of Tata Sons. The decision was taken at a board meeting held here today.
>
> The board has named Mr Ratan N. Tata as Interim Chairman of Tata Sons.
>
> The board has constituted a Selection Committee to choose a new Chairman.
>
> The Committee comprises Mr Ratan N. Tata, Mr Venu Srinivasan, Mr Amit Chandra, Mr Ronen Sen and Lord Kumar Bhattacharyya, as per the criteria in the Articles of Association of Tata Sons. The committee has been mandated to complete the selection process in four months.

Immediately, the news broke across all TV channels in India and spread like wildfire on social media. It was also reported that three members of Mistry's top team had been asked to put in their papers. While not the chairman of Tata Sons, Mistry was still a board member of Tata Sons and the chairman of the board of directors of most of the major group companies. The media started speculating whether Mistry would step down as chairman of these companies. This was intriguing since the first board meeting coming up was for Tata Global Beverages Limited (TGBL), to be held on 26 October at Bombay House.

CEOs being fired is always news, despite it not being a terribly uncommon occurrence. What made the firing of Cyrus Mistry so unusual was that the Tata group had a history of only six chairmen over 148 years! Cyrus Mistry was selected after a careful process that took over a year and by assuming the role at the age of forty-six, he was expected to serve from twenty to thirty years. Furthermore, just three months ago, the NRC (nomination and remuneration committee) of Tata Sons in their annual appraisal of Cyrus Mistry as chairman had given him a glowing review, with individual board members noting their appreciation of his performance. They recommended a higher raise than the 6 per cent that Cyrus was willing to accept, because that is what he had awarded the GEC members. In general, the Tata group was renowned for its values, which did not encompass a 'hire and fire' policy. Most senior Tata executives were consummate insiders, having usually served their entire career with the group.

The initial contract under which Cyrus was serving as the chairman had been passed via a shareholder resolution of Tata Sons. It was due to expire on 31 March 2017. Instead of the sudden, no-warning dismissal, the board could have just let the clock run out in five months. By eschewing the public humiliation of Cyrus Mistry, the bloody aftermath that followed could have been avoided. Unfortunately, instead there was the subsequent public airing of the underbelly of the Tata group as well as the deleterious impact on the reputations of Ratan Tata, Cyrus Mistry and the Tata brand. The market cap of Tata group companies fell by $13 billion in the seven weeks following the departure. The only winners as far as one could see were the public relations companies and lawyers, who are still having a field day.

Postscript

Let me just conclude that a year later, despite the best efforts of the press promoted by the six PR agencies and pressure from the internal Tata communications team, only two Tata CEOs, Bhaskar Bhat and Harish Bhat, have had anything negative to say about Cyrus Mistry in the press. And, even they were remarkably muted in their criticism. Under the circumstances, what better performance review could Cyrus Mistry have received as chairman of Tata Sons?

3

I Just Got Fired!

On taking over as chairman, Cyrus had taken a year to put his leadership team in place. Called the Group Executive Council (GEC), it comprised two old Tata hands (Harish Bhat and Mukund Rajan) and three members (Madhu Kannan, N.S. Rajan and myself) recruited from outside the group. Heading strategy for the Tata group, I interacted intensively with Cyrus as we formulated Tata's strategy until 2025.

My Blog: I Just Got Fired!

On the morning of 24 October, I recall asking Cyrus if he needed my help with the board meeting. I only attended Tata Sons board meetings to support Cyrus. This was when formal presentations on group strategy were scheduled, usually during the longer June and December meetings. Since governance rather than strategy was on the agenda, Cyrus said he could manage on his own. Anticipating this, I was scheduled with two of my GEC colleagues, Harish Bhat and N.S. Rajan, to be on a panel and take questions from around 100 young Tata executives on the group's big data initiative.

At 2. 50 p.m., we reached the Taj Hotel President property in Mumbai where the event was being held, completely unaware of the events at Bombay House. Our panel was being moderated by Deep Thomas, CEO of Tata iQ, the big data company. Enthusiastic participants were quizzing us. N.S. Rajan was looking at his phone and unexpectedly walked off the podium. He returned a few minutes later, ashen-faced, and whispered in my ear that the chairman has been asked to step down. My head jerked – what? Being on the panel, I kept answering the questions, but signalled to Deep that we needed to wrap this up early. NS looked very distracted and flustered so I fielded any questions that came his way as he soon left the podium and the room.

We walked out into the hall and N.S. Rajan informed Harish and me that his understanding is that with the chairman, all three of the outsiders on the GEC have also been let go. I invited them to my apartment for a drink rather than return to Bombay House until we gathered more information. Harish, as was his style, kept reassuring the two of us that the firing of Cyrus and the three GEC members was very unfair. We turned on the television and all the Indian television channels were plastered with Cyrus Mistry and three GEC members being asked to leave.

By 7.00 p.m., both my fellow GEC members had departed. I was unable to get hold of Madhu, usually my most reliable source of information. Finally, Ishaat Hussain responded by asking me for a drink at his place at 7.30 p.m. Ishaat was clear that he had no idea this was going to happen. He had entered the board meeting a few minutes late. Subedar, standing outside the board room, with a white face, had informed him that Cyrus was being fired.

At 9.00 p.m., I got a call from Subedar, with whom I had worked closely and got along rather famously as we were often on the same side of arguments. He came from a finance background, and I being a rational business school academic, both of us pushed for greater capital efficiency and performance orientation. Anyway, on this call, he simply said: 'It is my unpleasant duty to say your services are no longer required.' No explanation. I queried did this mean I did not need to show up the next morning? An affirmative reply, and that was it. Now readers, no pity is needed. It is something that has happened to many, and there are entire reality shows on television built around the theme 'You are fired!' Still, nothing prepares you for this. I realized that I was unemployed for the first time since the age of eighteen.

My first thoughts went to the seventy-plus people I had accumulated in the Big Data team over the past year. What was going to happen to them? They joined on my word that we were going to make this a core capability of the group. Quickly, I shot off a text message to a colleague with a plea to take charge of this venture. My four-member team I was less concerned about as they were enormously talented and familiar enough with the group to land on their feet.

Once fired, you discover your friends and the integral qualities of those who worked with you. The interesting insight for me was that the higher you go in the organization, this 'human' aspect declines. The people at the 'bottom' of the pyramid treated me with the same respect and affection as always. Their smiles were genuine and open. Those in the middle, like my team, were sincerely sad to see me go. They repeatedly mentioned what fun it was to have worked with me. It was not as if I was fired for non-performance (my last evaluation was excellent). I always do my best – it's the least I expect from myself and the most anyone can expect from me. I was fired for just being there at my position – working intensely and extensively with Cyrus.

The reaction at the top of the pyramid was interesting. With three exceptions, the many CEOs and top executives I worked with closely for three years went silent. I wonder what it is that the more we have, the more we become prisoners of the thought of losing it, rather than having it set us free. The lesson for my team was clear. I told them these people have made it to the top. They know how the system works. When in future anyone mentions me, please don't say anything positive. Throw me under the bus to gain credibility in the new regime. It's my parting advice.

Despite the unceremonious and un-Tata-like end, I have nothing negative to say about the Tata group. It was not the fault of the 675,000 Tata people and does not reflect on them. What I found exceptional about the group was the kind of person that Tata attracts – unpretentious and dedicated. Yes, they really drink, as we would say in America, the 'koolaid' of Tata. But I observed how hard they work, and how committed they are to the group and its values. They deserve a great chairman.

Finally, I really loved the job. It gave me, an academic, a ring-side seat to a 100+ billion-dollar group. Among the memorable things, the amazing discussions we had on what the group should look like in 2025, bouncing ideas back and forth, challenging each other and then coming to a joint view and understanding of the potential portfolio in 2025, after debating the trends and financial prospects. In my thirty-year career, I have had only three bosses who inspired me: Lou Stern, my PhD advisor at Northwestern University; Laura Tyson, my dean at LBS, and Cyrus Mistry.

The Response to 'I Was Just Fired!'

An old school friend advised me that in the Indian context, it is better not to mention I have been fired to anyone as it would have a deleterious impact on my reputation and job prospects. Better, he said, say 'resigned'. But, with my blog, 'I just got fired', much of which is reproduced above, I decided otherwise.

My rationale was simple. When I joined the Tata group, we decided not to make any announcements to the press or make me available to the press. Despite this strategy, the *Economic Times* managed a scoop by featuring my hiring by Cyrus Mistry for the Group Executive Council on their front page. Subsequently, the news appeared in almost every Indian newspaper of consequence. My feeling was that this coverage was garnered because of the content that I had delivered to the Indian press over the preceding decade via the seven books that I had authored. Well, if I had arrived with a big bang in the country, I was determined not to go silently into the night just because I was fired.

It was a surprise to see the scale of amplification of my post. It was picked by six major Indian newspapers for the front page of their print editions on Sunday. It was also reprinted on many websites. The blog website got more than 30,000 views with thousands sharing it on Facebook and LinkedIn. Twitter was alive for at least three days, with my profile obtaining 12,000 views and hundreds of new followers.

LinkedIn was where the blog found the most resonance. More than 100,000 views, 4,400 likes, 400 shares and 500 people taking the time to comment. I discovered that there is an entire community of people who have been fired and are looking for someone to verbalize their feelings. My blog gave them a voice. And, they appreciated it by sharing their personal stories with me. The humiliation they felt at being fired. The most heart-wrenching story was by a colleague of a man in the US who committed suicide after they were both fired. But there was optimism too. Many told me how being fired helped them change course, do the things they always wanted to do, reconnect with their families, work at helping others, start new businesses and, sometimes, end up in better jobs. Clearly, there is a potential TED talk called 'I Was Just Fired'.

The power of social media is interesting. It is hard to control when things go viral. On Facebook, Twitter and LinkedIn, the sentiment with respect to the comments was running 99 per cent plus in my favour. But, when the blog was published on major newspaper websites, it was less than 50 per cent. Why this difference, I wondered? On social media, for the most part, you are identified. In contrast, on a newspaper website's comments section, one can by posting a few anonymous comments change the direction of the commentary. The Tata group had employed six public relations firms to manage the fallout from the firing of Cyrus Mistry. However, social media is too vast to be controlled by any PR firm, especially when stories go viral in a big way. For this reason, it is understandably a very frustrating medium for traditional marketers and PR agencies seeking to manage their message.

Being an academic I believe in the power of ideas. I hope through this experience to teach others, who received the blog, that the pen is mightier than the sword. While it may seem at times that money and power are winning, history teaches us that no matter how many popes and kings had repeated that the earth was flat and the sun revolved around the earth, the truth, as it always does, won in the end. It may just seem like a long time while you are living it.

Over the week that followed the appearance of the blog, strangers came to me and said that they had read my blog. Sometimes, they shared a phrase or a sentence with their interpretation and complimented me on how deep it was. I wish I could take credit. But, to be honest, I wrote it in forty minutes while in 'flow'. I am not sure how much of it was conscious, from the head, versus from the subconscious.

As I indicated, it is in this type of situation that you discover your friends. I was touched by the outpouring of warm feelings and the belief that my friends, ex-students, and ex-colleagues had in my next act. Many who had not been in touch for some time sent me emails or messages. Altogether, I received at least 1,000 emails and other messages, if one includes those via Facebook, LinkedIn, and Twitter. Typical of these messages was:

'Wow, I just read your blog on being fired. I thought it was amazingly human, candid, moving and gracious at the same time. Very impressive. Obviously, a big shock, but your talents will no doubt turn it into an even bigger triumph. Let me know if I can be of any assistance with anything.'

It only reinforced what I learnt from my favourite Latin philosopher, Horace, who wrote in *Satires*: 'I live in the affection of my friends.'

4

Finding Resilience after Being Fired

As described in the previous chapter, the events on 24 October 2016 happened in rapid succession. Hearing Cyrus got fired at 5.00 p.m., learning from the television that I was let go at 6.00 p.m., and finally, the official phone call from Subedar at 9.00 p.m., asking me not to show up the next day. A few minutes later, Cyrus called. His voice was even lower than usual: Nirmalya, please let us finish dinner and then can we meet at my residence around 10.00 p.m. I summoned my chauffeur and told him to quickly have his dinner as we might be in for a long night.

It was the start of a furious two months, where I worked harder than ever with Madhu to help Cyrus wage a battle against the enormously powerful Tata machine until it moved to the courts. Enough studies have demonstrated that the biggest boost to resilience, the ability to bounce back from adversity, is through supporting others. Stung by the unfairness of the treatment meted out to Cyrus, I felt I had to aid his fight as it was our fight. This allowed me to avoid the usual depression that others might have experienced. I simply had no time to think about my future or get down on myself about the situation. Instead, having immediately hurled myself into the next task, it was part therapeutic, and part cathartic.

Of course, it helps to be blessed with an optimistic disposition. Considerable research indicates that optimism is a powerful trait. Rather than think I might never recover from this, at the back of my head, I knew that I would land on my feet. And, optimism, like pessimism, is contagious. When my daughter was informed that I was fired, she just rolled her eyes, probably thinking there is always some drama with dad, and remarked to her mother: it's dad, he will be fine. Optimism also helps lower the anxiety for those around you in the face of adversity.

Meeting the Challenge

Ultimately, what matters is how we interpret events that happen to us: the attributions we make for experienced adversity, how we frame the situation and consequently how we respond. One needs to transform the situation to one that is 'not personal, pervasive or permanent', as Adam Grant, the Wharton professor, once observed.

Making the appropriate attribution is beneficial to resilience. I did not blame myself for being fired. In my view, I was collateral damage in a situation where a person suffering hubris could not emotionally let go, despite having intellectually made the decision. In contrast, if you blame yourself, one can spend a lot of time in unproductive self-flagellation. Yet, one must balance this with extracting valuable lessons from the experience as well as not feeling helpless.

Instead of being depressed at losing a once-in-a-lifetime opportunity, my attitude was wow, I cannot believe that I even managed to do this in my career! It was natural, as an academic, to write my own story and convert the experience into a positive. It became a teaching moment. Beyond my defence, in the press, of Cyrus Mistry and the attack on the governance framework of Tata, I went to the leading business schools, including the IIMs in Bangalore and Calcutta, Indian School of Business in Hyderabad, S.P. Jain in Mumbai, INSEAD in Singapore, and London Business School, to present 'Living a Boardroom Battle'. Large audiences at these institutions engaged in a discussion of corporate governance practices, succession planning and the role of promoters in Indian business. The general feedback from these sessions was that I related the story factually and humorously, without any tinge of bitterness or vindictiveness.

Taking control of the narrative was important. Instead of letting what being fired said about me define interactions, by taking charge of the situation and reframing it, how I reacted became what defined me. As I was reflecting with a friend who was the chairman of a major Indian corporation many months later, he remarked: Nirmalya, you are the only person who came out a winner from the Mistry-Tata battle. To which, I added, 'and Chandra'.

I also used the time to pursue unfulfilled desires that a relentless schedule over the past twenty-five years had subverted. This led me to the three sacred sites of Bagan in Myanmar, Borobudur in Indonesia and Machu Picchu in Peru. These visits, which I called my pilgrimage, helped put things in perspective. We are but tiny specks in the story of humanity. At the end of the day, nothing is really that important.

Csikszentmihalyi, in his brilliant book, *Flow*, noted that people who achieve happiness do not regret the past, are reasonably satisfied with their lot in life, and look to the future with optimism. Given the opportunity to do it again, despite knowing the ultimate outcome, I would still jump at it. Of course, others who are fired may not be as fortunate as me, having fewer resources at their disposal. Once, my daughter complained, as teenagers often do, 'life is unfair'. I said yes, and it is unfair in our favour, or we both would not be sitting in business class seats from Europe to India. To cope with adversity, keeping an optimistic attitude, finding new challenges, helping others, reframing the situation and pursuing unfulfilled desires are effective strategies.

Long-term Effects

Being fired from such an exalted position, with such unexpectedness, for someone who has always previously experienced success, is distressing. And, it leaves traces on your soul. But, on reflection, that is okay. What is life, if not about ripening, evolving, into a more complete, more complex, individual. Incidents like this not only help in that journey, but also in developing greater empathy for others. By being more in touch with yourself and with others, one emerges, one hopes, as a better human being. As Victor Frankl, after spending three years in Nazi concentration camps out of which was born the path-breaking treatise *Man's Search for Meaning*, observed, 'what is to give light must endure burning.'

Section 2
Managing People

When teaching executives, if I asked them what the key success factors of any organization were, the most frequent answer was 'people'. As a rational academic, I found this deeply unsatisfying, as it revealed nothing except a black box. For me, having the right strategy, business model and implementation seemed to be much more important. People, as a vestige of my training in economics, I saw as simply a factor of production – a line on the graph.

Now after my experience in the corporate world, if you ask me what the most important discriminator was between those businesses I saw succeed and those that failed, my answer will be 'people'! Why this transformation? At Tata we had many companies, including fourteen that individually had a valuation of over $1 billion. At the group centre, the bandwidth to monitor even the top thirty companies that comprised 99 per cent of the group's valuation was limited.

What I observed was that if the right CEO was in charge, even if the company was in trouble, you could leave it alone. But if the 'right person' was not in the CEO chair, one had to constantly monitor the company, its performance, strategy, and so on. So, getting the appropriate CEO was the single most important factor for success, as subsequently, the strategy, business model and implementation could be then left to them with minimal oversight.

5

Are You a Prisoner or a Free Agent?

Getting hired and fired from Tata brought to life a concept that I used repeatedly in my teaching. It distinguishes between employees who are 'free agents' versus 'prisoners'. The concept flows from my research in the early 1990s on dependence, which was inspired by Emerson's famous 1962 paper in the *American Sociological Review*.[1]

Dependence of A on B is a function of the availability of alternatives. An employee's availability of alternatives to the present employer can be conceptualized as how long it would take to find another acceptable job and how much it would pay relative to the current compensation. Clearly, the faster

---

1. Richard M. Emerson (1962), 'Power-dependence relations,' *American Sociological Review*, Vol. 27, No. 1 (February), pp. 31–41.

one can find another job at a salary higher or similar, the less dependent one is on the current employer. This led me to place all employees in two buckets: those with high availability of alternatives, whom I dubbed as 'free agents', versus those with low availability of alternatives, or 'prisoners' in my terminology.

To keep things simple, I have selected compensation as the only factor. But one could add other aspects like job satisfaction, distance from home, or any other benefits that individuals receive from current and prospective employers.

Personally, one of the consequences of this conceptualization was to never negotiate too much on compensation. I always felt that too attractive a compensation package would turn me into a prisoner. My preference was to have the feeling that I could walk out any day if I didn't like my employment. And, this freedom is worth a few bucks to me as it lets me be who I am and fearlessly share what is on my mind.

In contrast, those who had worked themselves into becoming prisoners by negotiating too high a compensation must behave differently. They have little choice but to make public displays of loyalty to the organizational leader. I vividly recall a meeting where the CEO of one of our companies told Cyrus in front of a group of people present: 'Sir, my instinct is to always agree with you.' When the king is dead, such prisoners are the first to scream 'Long Live the King!'

Of course, the challenge is that some prisoners (perhaps, myself included) think that they are free agents. Such people can be hard to manage as they have a delusional evaluation of themselves. However, using my conceptualization, I found them relatively easy to manage. All that is necessary is to confront them by saying, 'You should do what is best for you if you feel under-appreciated here. I promise to write you a great recommendation letter.' Often, that is the last you hear them complain. Organizations are particularly susceptible to being populated by prisoners who believe they are free agents because it is hard to pinpoint how critical any individual is. The performance criteria for most executives is fuzzy and the ratio of individual's input to organizational output is unclear.

From a management perspective, managing free agents requires a different approach than managing prisoners. Using carrots or rewards to motivate free agents may work, but these methods will not be as effective as they are for prisoners. Sticks or threats, which are extremely efficacious against prisoners, at least in the short run, are useless when deployed against free agents. Free agents will simply leave the organization if their managers ask them to obey under the threat of punishment.

The seductiveness of using threats and punishments as a way of managing people lies in the efficiency of this strategy. Unlike promises and rewards, where if the employee complies, there is a cost to the organization (price of fulfilling the promise and giving the reward), threats and punishments have no such explicit costs associated. If people comply, there is no need to levy the punishment, so it seems free. Over time, though, threats and punishments have organizational costs in terms of declining morale and fostering a corrosive culture.

Rather than rewards and punishments, influencing free agents requires more elaborate strategies. To comply with instructions from superiors, free agents seek information and arguments in support of such requests. Free agents will query why they should do what they are being asked to. Beyond using expertise and information, referent power is also effective on free agents. Referent power exists when free agents view the person who is trying to influence them as inspirational. For referent power to operate, the free agent must look up to the executive seeking to gain compliance from them as this reduces counter arguments on the part of the free agent. The difficulty with expertise and referent power in organizational settings is that it does not always flow with hierarchical positions.

Over my career, I have observed that most managers prefer to be prison wardens rather than viewing themselves as coaches of star teams. You may have noticed that when sports teams do not perform, it is the coach who gets fired rather than the players. Coaches are easier to find than talent on the field. Brilliant coaches deploy expertise and referent power to influence their players instead of rewards and punishments. As they are bound by contracts and hard to replace, it is not easy to let players go. Furthermore, successful athletes are too rich at a young age, limiting the value of monetary incentives.

The academic environment has dynamics comparable to sports teams. Faculty, especially the stars, have tenure (lifetime employment) and annual raises tend to be relatively small compared to what one can earn via consulting assignments or speaking engagements. Thus, deans have limited reward and punishment powers. I once recall telling a dean that I do not respond to incentives because that is how rats in a cage are controlled.

Organizations contend that talent is critical to their success. But the relative proportion of free agents to prisoners necessary for success differs dramatically across organizations. One needs to reflect deeply on the business model and core competences to assess this.

Finally, each executive should reflect on one's own managerial style. If one has only managed prisoners, then has one really managed anyone? Once you remove the ability to reward and punish, I find that most managers become naked.

6

How Do Insiders and Outsiders Succeed in Organizations?

Prisoners versus free agents is only one way to classify executives populating an organization. Another fascinating difference that I observed was between 'insiders' and 'outsiders'. Insiders are those who have been with the organization for a long time; often their entire career has been with a single firm. Outsiders are those who have been hired to bring fresh ideas, competences, and blood into the organization. They help confront sacred assumptions as only an outsider will tell you that your child is ugly.

Compensation Differences

Insiders often complain that they are paid lower salaries compared to newly recruited outsiders. To bid the compensation above their market value, insiders must convince the firm that there is a credible threat of their departure. A credible threat is when the firm believes the insider would leave and wishes to retain them. In such a situation, firms are theoretically willing to pay their insiders above market value because of the costs associated with hiring and getting a replacement up to speed.

The problem for insiders is that despite their constant declarations of how much other firms desire them, companies know their insiders intimately. Through their long association, the firm is aware of the mobility barriers facing any particular insider. Besides the emotional costs of leaving a known environment, other mobility barriers may include geographical location, spousal employment opportunity, and reluctance to change schools for their children. Consequently, many insiders are unable to command a premium to their market value.

Of course, the argument above ignores the reality that insiders who have only worked within one company for decades lower their market value. Other firms are unlikely to hire them. Single-organization insiders, unless one has worked for aspirational benchmark companies such as General Electric, Google, Facebook, or Procter & Gamble, are often viewed as only being effective within the system they have grown up in. In a sense, a substantial proportion of insiders end up becoming prisoners.

In contrast, hiring an outsider will require offering above market compensation. The potential hire takes the risk of going from being an insider to an outsider. They leave an environment that they know and have mastered for one that is unknown. Therefore, a compensation difference is built in between insiders and outsiders. And, it favours the outsiders.

Companies know that hiring an outsider has risks associated with it. No hiring process is perfect and some mistakes will be made either in judging the capabilities of the outsiders and/ or their ability to fit in. From the company's perspective, this risk is only worth taking if the outsider is of substantially higher quality than the insiders available or brings along unique capabilities. This exacerbates the compensation differences between outsiders and insiders as, all other things being equal, the average market value of the former is higher.

Since it is a natural human tendency to feel undercompensated (see chapter 7: Should Data on Salaries Be Transparent?) and have positive illusions (see chapter 11: How Do We Perceive Ourselves?), the entry of high-profile outsiders may bring about considerable envy and heartburn in insiders. Outsiders may need to 'to walk on water' to justify their compensation. And, even walking on water may draw snide comments such as 'it's because she can't swim'.

My Experience

Recruited as an outsider, I worked with many organization insiders or 'lifers'. Two of these insiders were colleagues on the GEC, who adopted different approaches to interacting with me. One, whose responsibilities were in the domain where I am globally recognized as an expert, was respectful yet challenging. After some initial wariness on both our parts, I came to respect him. The other was very generous in his praise, often to the point of overt adulation that made me uncomfortable.

To make sense of my experience, I related my observations about insiders versus outsiders to my insightful ex-colleague, Professor Madan Pillutla, of London Business School. His response:

> *Insiders bring knowledge about how to work the levers of power and influence, understanding of tradition, deep connections with specific individuals, and a large support base as most people do not want change.*
>
> *What do outsiders have – expertise clearly; otherwise they would not have been hired. Insiders know that expertise gives more status than knowledge about working internal levers of power. This might be especially true for insiders like your two colleagues with outstanding academic achievements from many years ago because they crave being seen as experts. These insiders might initially attempt to learn from the outsider or attempt to coopt them. This might work well or turn to envy.*

The above observations led me to wonder:

- What are the personal qualities of the insider and outsider that lead to positive or negative effects?
- What are the situational factors (i.e., culture) that lead to positive or negative effects?

Posting this discussion on LinkedIn led R. Satish Kumar of Larsen & Toubro to make the following comments that I found myself agreeing with. While I have adapted his comments, the essence is unchanged:

1. The need to bring in an 'outsider' is because the manager felt there was a capability or competence gap internally. If

this need was felt by the majority of the team, blending in the 'outsider' is easier as the insiders will be more welcoming. However, if the outsider was brought without adequate preparation by the manager, it will be seen as a single person's decision. No matter how powerful the manager is, there is likely to be hidden resistance. The rest of the team adopts a 'I told you so' approach every time the outsider fails.

2. The personality of the outsider and humility play a major role. The outsider must take the time to understand the organization culture, power centres (formal and informal), and work on getting quick acceptance though demonstrated competence. However, too much hype about such demonstrated success is also likely to be viewed negatively. It may be better to assign the success initially to someone internally till the person is able to establish his acceptance and credibility within the organization.

3. 'Insiders' don't want to be seen as incompetent or demonstrably lacking capability. They want to be appreciated for their loyalty to the organization, which has limited their exposure to the wider world outside. They may not be the best in the world but they believe they are the best inside the organization.

Finally, in a much larger context, Senator Elizabeth Warren recalled a dinner conversation with Larry Summers, the Treasury Secretary under Bill Clinton. Summers told the Senator that she had a choice: She could be an insider or she could be an outsider. But, Summers said, she must understand:

Outsiders can say whatever they want. But people on the inside don't listen to them. Insiders, however, get lots of access and a chance to push their ideas. People – powerful people – listen to what they have to say. But insiders also understand one unbreakable rule: They don't criticize other insiders.[1]

1. Rana Foroohar (2016), *Makers and Takers: How Wall Street Destroyed Main Street*, p.310 (Penguin Random House).

7

Should Data on Salaries Be Transparent?

Salary data is confidential in most companies. But, this does not prevent, one could even say enhances, wild speculations about the compensation of individuals within a company. The *Financial Times* quoted Patty McCord, the ex-chief talent officer of Netflix, argue that in the age of transparency such salary information could perhaps be open since 'it's data like any other and we should be able to justify it'.[1]

Call me old-fashioned, but I disagree. Nothing generates more animated discussion within organizations than trying to guess how much others earn. A substantial amount of time is

---

1. Andrew Hill, 'Pay transparency is the last taboo in business,' *Financial Times*, 20 June 2016.

wasted in this way, at the expense of people doing their jobs. Proponents of pay transparency feel that information freely available across the company would put a stop to this wasteful speculation. In addition, companies would have to think harder about their compensation structures and make them logically defensible. It would also signal that the organization truly believes in openness and freedom of information. Who can be against all of this?

But revealing an organization's compensation data would be acceptable only if people had a realistic assessment of their own self-worth and accurate perceptions of the value they bring to the organization. Unfortunately, most people, to put it kindly, have positive illusions. Or, if I were to put it unkindly, large numbers are delusional on this front.

More than a decade ago, I wrote what was my favourite academic paper on reactions to perceived inequity in relationships.[2] Unfortunately, this paper failed as it has only garnered 193 Google citations after all this time. Yet it was a great learning experience because it required me to immerse myself in the literature on compensation and equity theory.

One theoretical option is to pay everyone the same as that would be consistent with the equality principle. However, people would find this rather unfair, with good reason, because it would not reflect differential contributions. In addition, equality would have a deleterious impact on motivation. As a result, we aim for pay equity, where compensation is consistent with contribution.

---

2. Lisa K. Scheer, Nirmalya Kumar and Jan-Benedict E.M. Steenkamp (2003), 'Reactions to perceived inequity in US and Dutch interorganizational relationships,' *Academy of Management Journal*, Vol. 46 (June), pp. 303–17.

According to the equity theory, people judge that they are being paid equitably when they perceive that the salaries they and others receive are proportional to their respective contributions to the company. When the outcome-to-input ratio is unequal, inequity raises its head. A person perceives negative inequity (being undercompensated) if her income-to-contribution ratio is less than that of others. In contrast, a person perceives positive inequity (being overcompensated) if her income-to-contribution ratio exceeds that of others.

As must already be obvious to the reader, contribution to the organization is just one benchmark in determining salaries and pay hikes. One has to also examine the market value of the person. Some people have high 'value in use', in that they make important contributions to the organization, but their outside alternatives may be of poorer quality.

Others may be in the opposite situation, where they have attractive alternatives to the firm, but their contributions within it may be judged to be less than those without such alternatives. As a result, beyond relative contributions to the organization, one also has to consider the market value of the person in setting the compensation.

Across studies, one observes that about 55 per cent of all people feel they are undercompensated – which means suffering negative inequity – while only 10–12 per cent think they are being overcompensated. The remaining third of the workforce feels that they are being fairly compensated.

Pay transparency would skew these numbers to a greater degree. One can always find another person in the organization with whom a comparison would lead one to feel undercompensated. This means that pay transparency would make the proportion of people feeling undercompensated increase from the 'normal' 55 per cent. Research has conclusively demonstrated that the larger the number of people feeling undercompensated in an organization, the lower is the employee commitment, morale and trust.

In this context, a faculty colleague once shared a story from an American public university where it was mandatory to reveal pay data to the public. Each year, the list of salary increases awarded to the different faculty was put in every faculty member's pigeonhole. In one particular year, a certain faculty member, on receiving the list, straightaway searched for the name of his rival. Realizing that his rival's raise was higher, the faculty member suffered a heart attack and had to be taken to the hospital in an ambulance.

As Gore Vidal observed, 'It's not enough merely to win; others must lose.' And that is why pay transparency, despite the best of intentions, will fail. To observe the deleterious effects of revealing salaries, one only has to examine transparency in CEO compensation, which is mandatory in many countries. If pay inequity in general causes much anguish in companies, the severance packages of CEOs can often exacerbate the conflict and even cause it to spill into public discourse.

8

Are Golden Parachutes for CEOs Justified?

There is a lot of angst, and sometimes justifiable anger, against the large severance packages made to departing CEOs. Previously, these severance deals of CEOs only came to light after their exit. However, since 2006, the Securities and Exchange Commission requires data on CEO compensation in the US to be transparent. Data is still hard to collate, but the average exit package (often referred to as 'golden parachute' in the popular press) for CEOs of S&P 500 companies appears to be two to three times their annual compensation.

A Google search of the ten largest golden parachutes reveals that $100 million just about gets you on the list, which tops at a whopping $417 million paid to Jack Welch of General Electric.

Yes, $417 million, and he left in a cloud because of the way he was said to have abused company perquisites for personal use. No wonder shareholder activists as well as many observers are outraged at these separation packages, especially when they are awarded to CEOs who have either served a short tenure or failed.

Even severance packages of successful CEOs are hard for the public to swallow. For example, Danny Vasella of Novartis was to be paid 72 million Swiss francs over six years, provided he did not go to work for the competition. This ignited an initiative banning such golden parachutes, which was put to Swiss voters as a public referendum. The Swiss, despite their pragmatism and business friendly attitude, still voted 68 per cent in favour of the ban. It was favoured by a majority in each of the twenty-six Swiss cantons.

I understand the public furore over this issue, and until recently had little sympathy for such CEO exit packages. However, at the risk of eliciting rebuke and derision, let me argue why I have had a change of heart on this issue. While one may legitimately question the amount awarded, there are sound reasons for the existence of golden parachutes for CEOs.

Most golden parachutes are negotiated by incoming CEOs who have been hired from outside the organization. One must realize that when hiring a new CEO, the pool consists of existing successful CEOs, unless it is an internal promotion.

An external candidate views the potential CEO opening as a risky proposition. Here you are, a successful CEO, comfortable in the organization you are leading, having negotiated the rules of engagement with important stakeholders. Now you are presented with an option in which you do not know the company, its problems, the depth of management, or the board of directors and their quirks.

Yes, the interviewing process yields some information, but as has been famously quipped, an interview is a conversation between two liars. The candidates present themselves as great and the company itself as perfect.

To accept the risk of leaving a known devil for an unknown one, it is not surprising that the incoming CEO negotiates a golden parachute. This is especially true if the previous CEO was fired, as it signals to the incoming CEO that this board has a penchant for letting CEOs go. Furthermore, in the euphoria of having found their 'man', the board and the recruitment committee are happy to agree to a golden parachute because it has no immediate cost to the company. In any case, at this stage of the process, the possibility of the incoming CEO's exit is furthest from their mind.

Boards of directors get most of the blame for excessive CEO pay. In my experience, many boards are easily manipulated by the CEO if the CEO has occupied that position for a few years. Yet, there is at least one rational reason for a CEO golden parachute from the shareholders' perspective. It makes the CEO less likely to stand in the way of the company being potentially acquired. As we know from the literature on acquisitions, being acquired is value accretive for the shareholders as the acquirer pays a premium for this privilege. The last thing a shareholder in the target company wants is the CEO worrying about their own future, and therefore, putting a spanner in the works. In most cases, the CEO of the acquired company will end up becoming unemployed.

Finally, CEOs hold a lot of sensitive information on the company. Regardless of how well-run and ethical the organization may have been, there are always skeletons in the closet. As I have frequently observed, let us not forget that within the space of a day we are all both sinners and saints. No one is perfect and it does not help to reify organizations or individuals. The silence of the outgoing CEO is valuable and more likely if the separation is on friendly terms.

To comprehend the costs of an unamicable CEO exit, one only needs to observe the $13 billion market cap decline for Tata group listed companies in the seven weeks after Cyrus Mistry was unceremoniously removed as chairman of Tata Sons. I do not wish to be misunderstood. Please note that the monetary terms of his exit were not an issue for Cyrus Mistry. I am simply using the incident to draw the more general conclusion that it is in the best interests of the shareholders for CEO exits to be as non-controversial and amicable as possible. The potential erosion of billions of dollars in shareholder wealth puts into perspective CEO golden parachutes that run into millions of dollars.

9

Can Employee Turnover Be Positive?

One of the benefits of being an academic is being surrounded by exceptionally intelligent individuals who have spent their entire life making sense of a single subject. And, they eagerly share this knowledge if you demonstrate any interest in their work. It has been my good fortune to have interacted, and even collaborated, with several such experts. Furthermore, academics love to debate. We are natural sceptics of any received wisdom, and, as such, push each other to think even more deeply. The result is that random conversations can lead to new insights for both parties.

Prabhakant Sinha was one of my professors at Kellogg when I was pursuing a PhD. Later, he was my colleague at London Business School when we jointly conducted an executive education programme on sales force. He is the most insightful person on sales force that I know, having both built a large consulting practice called ZS Associates and authored several excellent books on the subject. Since we faced some issues with sales force performance in several Tata companies, I invited Prabha to conduct a seminar. I took the opportunity of his visit to introduce him to Cyrus. We had an animated conversation on sales force attrition. While I cannot recall the exact conversation, it led to several insights for me on the topic of employee turnover.

Often, it is assumed that employee turnover in an organization is a negative signal of problems. To stem this attrition, simple solutions are proposed such as increasing compensation or looking at quality of life indicators in the organization. The latter is to determine if something in the culture of the organization is corrosive and causing employees to flee.

Who Is Leaving?

The big insight that Cyrus and I obtained from our evening with Prabha was that employee turnover data of a company is meaningless without the associated performance data that allows one to examine who is leaving the firm. Specifically, a closer examination of the profile of employees departing the organization can lead to the following nuanced conclusions:

- If the employees departing are generally 'poor' performers and the organization had classified them on entry as being low potential, then there is a recruitment problem. Clearly, the wrong people are being hired and one needs to examine the issues around recruitment such as the talent pools being searched, the criteria for selection, and the compensation offered.

- If the employees departing are generally 'poor' performers but the organization had classified them on entry as high potential, then there is an onboarding problem. Fix the training for new recruits and the coaching (such as assigning mentors initially to new recruits), as new recruits are not being supported adequately post hiring.
- If the 'high' performers are leaving, then first one must accept that a certain number of high performers will depart. This is especially true for those industries and/or functions where mobility is high because company-specific skills are relatively few. It is tempting to increase compensation to reduce attrition of high performers; while such an action may help at the margins, it is not a panacea. Generally, the employees being classified as 'high performers' are already well paid. Furthermore, in any case, other recruiters seeking to attract them would automatically match any increase. The answer here, albeit not a silver bullet, is availability of career advancement opportunities as well as providing them adequate recognition and appreciation.
- If everyone is leaving, then of course there are fundamental culture and strategy problems in the organization.

When to Encourage Employee Attrition?

In certain industries, firms want to encourage people to leave after some time because of the cost pressures. For example, in the airline (or retail) industry, companies like Southwest Airlines started with the lowest cost structure in the industry. But, over time, inevitably their costs rise as the employees become more experienced and older. The annual raises and the increased health care costs for older employees lead to creating a space for a new entrant. The result is the birth of Jet Blue, which hires younger people at lower cost. Clearly, this is because in the airline industry, employee costs are substantial while the other costs (fuel, airplanes) are remarkably similar across different competitors.

Of course, older employees making higher wages would not be a problem if experience, which is what age represents, brought greater employee productivity. The problem in industries such as retail, hospitality and airlines is that most of the workforce are engaged in front-line jobs where greater experience does not often lead to superior performance or productivity (the number of crew on a plane is unchanged regardless of experience). If anything, employees get jaded over their tenure and the quality of the customer service they deliver declines. One always worries if seniority determines who gets promoted to serve business class and first-class passengers in an airline. Please note, I am not implying that a rookie hired yesterday is as good or productive as a person with experience. Rather that the marginal returns to experience flatten rather quickly, and may even decline at some stage for a large proportion of the employees.

Realizing that experience may represent higher costs rather than higher productivity or performance, there are companies in such industries who, as part of their talent management strategy, encourage people to leave after a few years of service. They even help them with outplacement. Or in the case of Starbucks, with college education assistance. The hope is that after some college education, the employees will voluntarily depart for greener pastures.

10

Would You Trust a Robot?

As managing people is always a challenge, companies are increasingly enamoured by robots. For example, the biggest constraint on Uber's growth is the availability of drivers. No wonder they are investing heavily in driverless cars.

Initially, robots were designed to look and work like humans. This was the image from popular comics when I was growing up. However, now that robots have become mainstream, most robots are very unlike humans, and that is their strength. Let me explore this thought.

Are Robots Mainstream?

The answer to the question depends on what you see as a machine with artificial intelligence. Everyone reading this book has used an ATM machine to withdraw cash. And, this is how robots differ from the comic book concept. The best robots do one thing rather well. They are single-purpose machines like the ubiquitous robotic arms in factories.

Industrial robots have diffused rapidly in countries facing declining working age population and young people who do not wish for a factory career. In 2013, China became the leading buyer of industrial robots. By 2016, China had the largest installed base of industrial robots in the world. Yet, China has only thirty-six robots per 10,000 manufacturing employees compared to Germany with 292, Japan with 314, and South Korea with 487 robots per 10,000 manufacturing workers. These industrial robots look nothing like human beings.

Intelligent Robots

Artificial intelligence has now moved the focus from industrial robots working on preprogrammed repetitive tasks in enclosed spaces to robots that can adapt to changing conditions (i.e., learn) and interact with humans.

Just as industrial robots don't look like humans, robots with artificial intelligence don't think like humans. The original effort to build a machine that could beat a chess player began by interviewing grandmasters in the hope of having them articulate how they play and then fusing that logic into the computer. Well, as we have always known in marketing, consumers are clueless when it comes to explaining why they chose a certain brand. Similarly, experts were useless when asked to describe how they played chess so well. You got the same vacuous answers that you get from managers on what makes them successful – intuition and experience!

The breakthrough victory of Deep Blue, IBM's supercomputer, over the then world champion, Garry Kasparov, was based on sheer processing power combined with massive data storage capability. Similarly, Google's AlphaGo recently beat the champion Lee Sedol in four out of five games of Go without mimicking the ways champions play. Instead, these victories were achieved by approaching the task differently than humans through what is now called deep learning. These are machine learning algorithms that rely on an endless trial and error method to improve their performance on a task.

While Japan and Germany dominate the industrial robotic industry, China and USA are racing to dominate the deep-learning robotic space. China led in the patents related to robots with 35 per cent of all the patents filed in 2015. This was double that of the next highest country, Japan. Clearly, China has hardware capabilities second to none. However, because of its software expertise, USA is the real leader as robots become increasingly more software- than hardware-focused in character, driven by deep learning.

The victories of Deep Blue and AlphaGo, as impressive as they are, were still on tasks with defined rules requiring processing power. The challenge that remained was to succeed on tasks that require a combination of deep expertise and manual dexterity. Surgery seems to be just such a problem. Which is why STAR, a robot, outperforming surgeons in 2016, received so much attention. When tested on piglets (pigs apparently have an internal system which is close to humans), with minimal human intervention, the robots were found to have done more evenly spaced stitches that resulted in less leaky sutured guts. The researchers now claim to have managed to make STAR work autonomously.

The Challenge of Robots

The advantages of robots over humans are easy to comprehend. Using them reduces variance in the performance of the task (greater precision as there are no mood swings or distractions), the ability to work in hazardous conditions, and, most of all, absence of the many demands that humans make such as pay raises and coffee breaks. Still, as robots increasingly interact with humans, it might be fruitful to think of three potential situations:

1. You are flying on an airplane with no pilot, essentially a drone.
2. You are in an autonomous vehicle, where there are no controls to manipulate.
3. You are under surgery and being operated on by a robot.

In these situations, would you trust robots? And, if something went wrong, who would be accountable?

It brings to the forefront the special domain still considered human – creativity, feelings, empathy and the ability to exercise judgement. People would not feel comfortable, for example, for a programmed car to make the decision on whether it should let the impeding vehicle go unharmed since the latter has four occupants, while allowing the death of the lone rider in the autonomous car (assuming only one vehicle can be preserved). Keeping humans in the loop makes robots more socially acceptable, which is why we would insist on having a pilot on the plane, a surgeon in the operating theatre and the ability for the occupant to override the autonomous car.

Speaking of feelings, people can fall in love with robots. When asked if it is better than falling in love with a person, an insightful researcher replied 'No, but what if you don't have that option?' This leads me to end with the story from 1963 when Luther Simjian filed a patent for an ATM machine that allowed deposits. On the ATM failing the pilot test in New York and being discontinued after six months, Simjian reflected:

'The only people using the machine were a small number of prostitutes and gamblers who didn't want to deal with tellers face to face.'[1]

Disruptive change does not follow a predictable pattern.

---

1. Ben Ikenson (2004), *Patents*, New York: Black Dog & Leventhal.

11

How Do We Perceive Ourselves?

While a professor at IMD – International Institute for Management Development – in Switzerland, I was the co-director of the Programme for Executive Development, which targeted senior managers in their forties and fifties who had been successful in their careers in a functional role. Overwhelmingly, they did not have an MBA, as it was not a common degree in continental Europe in the 1970s and 1980s. They were sent to the programme because their company now desired them to take a general management role. This was one of the best teaching experiences of my career as it taught me a lot about business and general management. It was a ten-week full-time programme, and by the time I let it go, ran four times a year with seventy-five participants from about thirty different countries.

During the programme, one of the most impactful interventions was on the Friday afternoon of the first week of the programme. By then, the programme had run five days and seventy-five successful managers, 80 per-cent-plus male, had behaved as they usually do. The intervention was simple: they were to go to their small (6–7 people) study groups with whom they had been working over the past week. I wanted the participants to take turns and tell each of the other participants the one thing they wished the other participant did more of, and one thing that they did less of. They were to focus on behaviours only, not attitude. The person receiving the feedback was not allowed to interrupt, but could request a clarifying example in case they had not fully understood the feedback. For most of the participants, this was the first honest feedback they had received in their careers. Those providing the feedback were successful peers with no axe to grind. If they chose, they could avoid interacting with these people again as the study groups changed each week.

Johari Window

When they returned after an hour, I would put up the Johari window that describes the public, private, blind, and unknown self.

The discussion that followed usually brought out several points including:

- A smaller private self is not always a bad thing as some people are more private than others. We all have at least an implicit theory of 'who I allow myself to be in the world'. But, such an exercise helps realize that we are each more than what we allow – both from the perspective of what we keep hidden

Feedback
Self-Disclosure Matrix

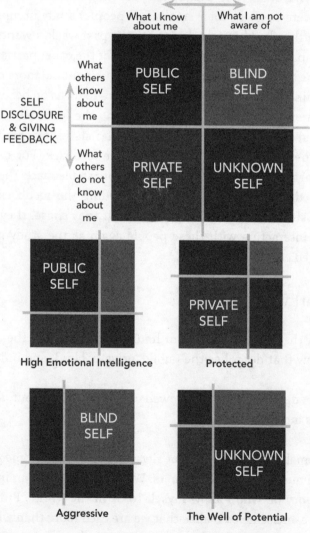

Adapted from: https://en.wikipedia.org/wiki/Johari_window

from others and what information we believe we let others see. The feedback leads to the understanding that we are all more naked than we thought we were.

- Unlike a small private self, a smaller blind self and unknown self are always preferable. Each of us has a blind self which we need to be aware of as we go about our careers since this is what contributes to others' perception of us. And, of course, the size of this blind self depends on one's self-awareness.

- As has been often noted, we judge ourselves by our intentions, but we judge others by their behaviour. This Johari window in groups leads to the awareness that others are more profound and complex than our perception of them.

Since most of us have positive illusions about ourselves, the Johari window helps us confront the gap between our beliefs of ourselves and what others think. If this gap becomes too large, then we feel undervalued and misunderstood. For example, I recall a conversation in the Tata executive lunch room. An executive, the consensus about whom was that he was most 'political', proclaimed that the only kind of managers he found difficult to work with were those who were political. This led to silence in the room as the other six or seven colleagues looked at each other, flummoxed as to what to say next. Finally, after a pause and unable to resist, I said, 'Well, there is a difference between how we perceive ourselves and how the world perceives us.' Now, it may be that he was not delusional, but just attempting some good old-fashioned impression management. Regardless, the Johari window is a powerful psychological concept, which is helpful in seeking as well as interpreting feedback. Each of us can benefit from reflecting and applying it to ourselves. If no one else is around, I suggest asking your spouse or children for feedback. It will be revealing. As Robert Burns observed in his poem in 1786:

'O wad some Power the giftie gie us
To see oursels as ithers see us!'

The Art of Seduction

Thinking of how we perceive ourselves, someone once told me that Machiavelli said the art of seduction is telling good-looking people they are intelligent, and intelligent people they are good looking. I have no idea if Machiavelli expounded on this subject, but the advice is truly Machiavellian. Often, when I observe how men behave around women, it appears to me that men would be better advised to reflect on this Machiavellian prescription.

For example, consider the incident that occurred once as I was strolling in the Knightsbridge neighbourhood of London, a particular haunt of beautiful people, especially around the department stores of Harrods and Harvey Nichols.

Alongside me passes an extremely attractive woman. A guy walking towards us calls out to her: 'Hello, gorgeous!' As would be expected, she ignores him. She looks towards me as a way to avoid him. I just roll my eyes.

The man, after passing, turns around to see if she has reacted. Yes, folks, after millions of years of evolution, and including such inane actions as tooting the car horn, these are some of the best mating strategies men have thought of.

Think about it. Hasn't she heard since she was a baby how good looking she is? Probably her tragedy is that people don't look past that to discover her other qualities. Much more effective, I think, to focus on those.

Brands: Target Versus Reflection

Consumer brands are in the business of seducing clients by playing on their perceptions of themselves. Our favourite consumer brands help us to express how we would like to see ourselves, and how we would like others to see us. The beauty industry advertising reflects this.

The aspirational aspect of cosmetics with its celebrity endorsements is demonstrated by companies like L'Oréal. Each brand in this aspirational business must specify two sets of consumers. The first is the 'target', which comprises of the segment of consumers that the brand expects will buy its products. The second is 'reflection', or the segment of consumers that the 'target' segment believes consumes the brand, much more upmarket from a demographic (income, class) perspective.

The advertising for the brand features endorsers from the 'reflection' segment. As a result, the target segment sees its reflection in this, more aspirational, set of people. This advertising is persuasive, regardless of whether consumers believe that the endorsers are actual consumers of the brand that they are pitching. For example, I doubt that most consumers think Beyonce is using L'Oréal lipstick, wearing H&M clothes, or drinking Pepsi, all brands that she has endorsed.

Everyone is trying to be someone they are not.

12

Does Experience Matter?

The executive lunch room at Bombay House led to interesting conversations. During a discussion there, an elder colleague of mine, whom I admired, mentioned that he was very aware that when he was young, he felt that the older colleagues were not in touch with tomorrow. As a result, now that he is older, he lets young colleagues frequently try different things even if he may not always see the wisdom in them. This is something I endorse strongly. As a young, upstart faculty member, I often rolled my eyes at my older colleagues. Then I became one of them.

With age, we must start questioning to what extent our experience matters. And, when and where? You can see this question play out with large human consequences as young people cannot get jobs because they don't have any experience and the over fifties, especially in Western economies, cannot get a job because of age discrimination.

Experience, of course, implies knowledge and an ability to do a job because of the learnings of the past. I would prefer a doctor, surgeon, pilot, nuclear power plant operator and so on with experience. Similarly, I would not give my money to a money manager unless they have lived through a recession and a long bear market. On the other hand, experience may imply rigidity and not keeping up with the latest techniques, such as with a surgeon. Experience, from a knowledge perspective, is only relevant if it also implies continuous learning.

Then there is the freshness of youth. Youth implies creativity, energy, drive and ambition and a reckless 'go for it' attitude, no matter the odds. Henry Ford summarized this argument:

> *It is not always easy to get away from tradition. That is why all our new operations are always directed by men who have no previous knowledge of the subject and therefore have not had the chance to get on really familiar terms with the impossible.*

As we stand, technology is changing our world and our relationship to it is dependent on our age. If, like me, you are in your fifties, you remember the day when a PC was brought in to your workplace (1984) and to your home (1986 – my first IBM PC and I had to buy the extra 64K of memory for 125 dollars to get it to 128k). I started with Lotus 123 and Word Perfect and saw Internet and email come into my life in 1990. Yes, I have achieved a certain level of mastery of this world in order to survive.

Contrast this experience with that of someone in their late thirties or forties who grew up with computers, though probably only got a mobile phone after graduating from college. The technology is part of their life. Now think of someone in their twenties or even my daughter who is sixteen. She is probably on her fifth smart phone and does not know what a house/life without a computer, internet, or smart phone looks like (albeit the first smart phone at home when she was born was a Blackberry). She is a digital native – for her, technology is like a mother tongue rather than a second language.

Experience and Functional Expertise

The impact of experience on different organizational functions differs. Imagine I am hiring a chief financial officer (CFO) or chief legal officer or a head of factory operations. Experience is good here. Yes, technology has changed, but for their job, the important things are unchanged. A CFO several years in the job knows how to manage the auditors, has built good relationships with important external stakeholders, and provided they keep up with the changing reporting and financial regulations, experience is only positive.

Similarly, an experienced corporate lawyer knows the company's history, the past and present litigations, the corporate structures and existing agreements. The law changes rather slowly, and if they keep abreast of these changes, I would prefer experience over youth. The factory manager who has been there a long time (unless it is a drastic turnaround situation) knows the factory well and the pressure points for obtaining further efficiency gains as well as the bottlenecks. All good so far.

In contrast, consider I want to hire a chief marketing officer and my challenge is to move quickly to new marketing and media channels where the youth are currently residing. If we need to embrace Facebook, Twitter, Pinterest, Instagram,

Snapchat, Whatsapp and Kik, who am I going to hire? What is the advantage of experience over youth here?

Forget someone in their fifties; even a forty-five-year-old may be too old. It may be that we discriminate in favour of the late twenty-year-old. I know this is harsh, but marketing is the place where technology is really having an impact. It is where 'core capabilities' are being transformed into 'core rigidities'. Of course, with a voracious learning attitude, a fifty-plus person can comfort themselves by saying that it is not age or experience that matters, but mindset. However, it will take an exceptional person in their fifties who has mastered the new technology landscape.

Section 3

Managing Teams

The academic world is a high IQ world where people work alone for long hours. Collaboration with other colleagues is by choice. In general, most of the collaborations happen with co-authors who are usually located at other universities in the world. As a result, faculty members tend to identify themselves more with the community of professors in their field rather than with the institution they are presently at. While I have been at six universities over my career, my primary identification with marketing professors worldwide through associations and conferences has remained unchanged.

Beyond research, teaching is also done as an individual in front of a class. With the exception of teaching core marketing at Harvard Business School, I was always responsible for independently developing and delivering any courses. Whatever the success or failure of a course, it was entirely my responsibility. Therefore, EQ (emotional intelligence) is not something that is particularly valued in academic circles. Faculty have a well-deserved reputation for being loners and difficult to work with. In this sense, they are like artists.

If you are a lone player with great talent – like a sportsperson or an artist or painter – you are then free to work alone, without regard to what the world thinks of you. You have no responsibility, except to hone your own talent – to become the best in the world, and to strive for excellence. It's a lonely journey, where you learn to practise hard and live your own failures.[1]

The corporate world, on the other hand, works in teams, where collaboration and cooperation are key to achieving any outcome. Self-awareness and the ability to manage others are critical ingredients for success. As an academic thrust into the corporate world, intellectually I understood the importance of EQ for success, but, it was not my natural playing field. And, as the same article that I quoted from above so eloquently observed:

If you've chosen to be a manager, you've then got to be among people, collaborate with them, lead them or be led by them, be able to handle their frustrations, to handle their competence and their incompetence. It's an ego-crushing journey where you need to learn to allow people their space to work. It has very little to do with intelligence – it is more about developing sensitivity – finding a way to motivate people, to pull them in one direction. A journey of frustration, but equally one of triumph when you see the team working together and winning – a journey you share with your team.

More frequently than one would like, seeking what was 'rationally' the best decision for the business could be sub-optimal from a personal survival perspective. I do not think I fully adapted to my new environment and

---

1. Harsh Chawla, 'The Rahul Yadav story you've never heard before,' https://www.foundingfuel.com/article/the-rahul-yadav-story-youve-never-heard-before (accessed on 23 March 2018).

appreciated this point. Still, as this section will, I hope, demonstrate, I did devote considerable thought to the problem. If only practice was as easy as theory.

As businesses become multinational in scope, the challenge of managing teams becomes more complex. While it may seem exciting, managing multicultural human resources taxes even the most savvy of managers. At Tata, the operations were multinational, with 70 per cent of the revenues from outside India. But we struggled to widen the participation of other nationalities in the top management.

13

Is There Too Much Talent in the Team?

Something I have often reflected on is whether there can be too much talent on a team. For a team to succeed, each individual needs to perform and the team needs to collaborate effectively. Whether a team can have too much talent rests on the extent to which the task requires collaboration, or what we academics call 'high interdependence'.

To elaborate on the concept of interdependence in team contexts, I used to distinguish between two types of sports. There are those team sports, like cricket or baseball, where the coordination required between team members is relatively minimal. Then there are the second type of team sports, like basketball, hockey or soccer, where real-time and continuous coordination between members is necessary for team success.

The point is that the relative importance of the two components, individual performance and collaboration, depends on the type of sport. For example, in cricket, interdependence and coordination is limited to largely running between wickets. As a result, individual talent is more important than collaboration between team members. In contrast, hockey, soccer and basketball are sports in which people play with each other as much as against each other. This is especially the case for basketball, where a few players coordinate intensively on a rather small court.

Recently, I found an academic study that tested and documented what was my informal hypothesis. Professor Adam Galinsky with his co-authors studied team success during ten seasons of baseball and basketball.[1] In baseball, which, like cricket, requires relatively low coordination between players, the more the talent on the team, the higher the performance of the team. In contrast, in basketball, team performance improves with better talent, but only up to a point. Beyond a certain level, adding more talent to a team led to lower team success. In basketball, at higher levels of talent, the detrimental effects on team performance from decline in collaboration could not be offset by the individual performance benefits that the additional talent brought to the team.

To summarize, adding more talent to cricket teams will always help. However, adding more talent to a hockey, football, or basketball team may not always lead to better results. Unfortunately, there is no formula for knowing when the point of too much talent has been breached in high interdependence teams. Ultimately, it is the coach's call to assess that, and to

---

1. Adam Galinsky and Maurice Schweitzer (2015), *Friend & Foe: When to Cooperate, When to Compete, and How to Succeed at Both* (Crown Business).

ensure that the range of skills needed are present on the team, without getting in the way of status conflict harmful to team performance.

Interesting research from farms can help enlighten our understanding of status conflict from talent and its deleterious effects on team performance. Any farmer would like to have the highest egg-producing chickens together on the farm. But studies indicate that this results in egg production actually declining. Why? The highest egg-producing chickens are also more competitive and dominant. As a result, when placed together, they start battling for territory and status. This fight for pecking order distracts the chickens from producing the most eggs. Similar animal spirits are alive in us, and only sometimes, below the surface in organizations.

Conclusion

When I was growing up, I felt that India for years had eleven of the best hockey players in the world but were beaten by teams with relatively average players who worked harder on team concepts and team techniques (e.g., penalty corners). Having worked in more than sixty countries as a consultant, I have discovered that some cultures excel at team work. This is especially true of smaller countries such as Netherlands and Sweden, but also for some larger countries like Germany, Japan, and Thailand. In India, the team concept is hard to make work as people dislike playing their position. Walk into a retail setting, and one will observe employees get in each other's way rather than staying at their stations, or jointly do tasks that are more effectively done by an individual.

This brings me to the question of whether in organizations we think deeply enough about which type of team sport is the relevant analogy when forming teams and incentivizing them. The questions that should be reflected on are:

- In which tasks do we need high interdependence for success, and in such situations, how do we select the 'best talent' for the team? How do we trade-off 'best' talent or individual performance with 'best for the team' or collaborative performance?
- In which tasks is the level of interdependence rather low (clear roles can be defined with strict interfaces) and how do we ensure we have the best talent for these teams?
- Does the definition of who is the 'best talent' differ when we work in these two situations? Are we discerning enough?

The important point is that companies have very strong models to allocate cash (financial capital) to projects and manage portfolios of projects with different risk/reward profiles. But, we have relatively poor models to allocate people (human capital) to teams.

14

Can You Mentor Someone Better Than Yourself?

Finding success in professional life is challenging. You are alone, competing against others, many of whom are smarter than yourself. One needs all the help one can get. If, by chance, someone takes enough interest to become a mentor, then one is indeed fortunate.

A mentor, by definition, is someone dedicated to the growth and success of the other – the mentee. It is this empathy that leads to a relationship of trust on the part of the mentee and the dedication of effort on the part of the mentor. Mentors are usually more experienced, more knowledgeable about the profession and inspirational to the mentee. Some people, I suspect most, never experience what it is like to have an explicit mentor guide their development. On the other hand, if you are as lucky as I have been, you found more than one exceptional mentor over your career.

When Do You graduate?

For academics, usually one's PhD advisor is a mentor. At Northwestern University, I was adopted by Lou Stern. Lou was an exceptional scholar. But, he was also an amazing teacher with a prolific speaking and consulting practice. He inspired me to view being an academic as more than research and teaching, but also to impact practice at the highest levels.

Given that I was a mere doctoral student, the power differential between us was gigantic. At the start, I could not imagine having a career as successful as his. Since he was very demanding, I was always hesitant to present my paper to him, fearing that it would not meet his high standards. And, Lou, while never personal in his criticism, did not feel shy of observing the limitations of anyone's paper, no matter how famous or accomplished they were.

Good mentors not only inspire, but help growth through specific, actionable and timely feedback. Any paper submitted to Lou was returned full of comments on where the arguments were weak, how to improve and what he found interesting. I recall once having worked tremendously hard for two months on a paper before placing it in his mailbox early one morning. Thinking I would take the day off, I started to head out after answering a few emails, only to find the first fifteen pages extensively marked up by Lou in my mailbox.

On my dissertation under his supervision, we must have had at least a hundred iterations before it was finally successfully defended by me and the resulting paper published. Mentors dedicate enormous time and energy. It is also a risky venture, as some mentees develop, while others stagnate, to the frustration of the mentor who saw greater potential.

After obtaining my first position as professor, I started another research project with Lou. We submitted the paper to a leading journal, only to have it rejected. Believing there was a case for reconsideration, Lou told me to write the first draft of the appeal and then he would look at it before sending it off to the editor. On my contention that I could manage this on my own, he said no, he always needed to have a final look. I formulated the draft of the two-page, single-spaced appeal letter to the editor. Lou read it, added one comma, and then looked at me and said: 'You don't need me any more.' We never worked again on a project. Based on the absorptive capacity of the mentee, great mentors know when it is time to cut the cord.

The Inadvertent Mentor

Two of my mentors, John Mason and Jacques Horovitz, never intended to be mentors, perhaps they were even unaware of it. This is significant. If one can be a mentee without the mentor knowing, or acquiescing to it, a whole world of mentors unlocks.

All the way to high school, I was an average student with, at best, middling grades. The reason was not hard to fathom, as I never did the assigned homework. I still do not have a good explanation as to why, except that I have a visceral adversarial reaction to authority figures and being told what to do.

About six months before high school was coming to an end, one day, for some inexplicable reason, I decided to hand in the homework assignment. Next day, my classroom teacher, the legendary John Mason, when returning the graded assignment asked me to stand up in front of the class. Then he proceeded to read my submission to the class. After that he declared that he believed I would top the upcoming high school external examinations. The class looked on in disbelief. But, through that one act, he changed my life. We interacted daily until I graduated from high school, but then lost touch.

Fast forward thirty-five years, through Facebook, I get in touch with John Mason. Explaining that I am an ex-student from La Martiniere, I invited him for lunch when I was next in Delhi. Over lunch, I recounted several stories and lessons from his class. He gently observed that while he recalled several batch mates of mine, especially the exceptional ones, he had no recollection of me. Such is the inadvertent potential power of mentors to transform lives.

Managing Someone Better Than Yourself

When I was teaching at IMD, I came up with the observation that following a great leader is easy as it is so motivating. But it does not happen too often. Being a great leader is difficult as it is about enhancing the opportunities for others, or why should anyone follow you? But, the hardest is managing someone who is better than yourself and is going places that you will never reach. This is where most of us fail. It does not have to be this way.

One should be able to accept that some people, who are both younger and not as high in the hierarchy, are simply better. I had just such an experience when collaborating on the *India Inside* book with my friend Phanish Puranam. Phanish is at least ten years younger than me and was then a recently tenured associate professor. In contrast, I had been a full professor for more than a decade.

Early in the project I realized I was with someone better than myself. At the book launch party, with the London Business School dean in attendance, I reflected on the rules I had developed for working with someone better than yourself:

1. Don't try to compete as you will lose.
2. When they say they are going to do something, try not to get in the way as you will make the outcome worse.
3. Always keep in mind that they are going on to bigger and better things. But, you were privileged to have shared a part of their journey, however briefly.

One of the great lines I heard from C.K. Prahalad, when we once shared a stage together in Abu Dhabi for a client, was: 'Break Rules, Build People.' What a wonderful motto.

15

Do We Need Multicultural Teams?

While many companies are multinational, most of the top management teams (TMTs) in these companies are not. They tend to be dominated by executives with a connection to the home country of the company. While there is a lot of attention paid to gender diversity, cultural diversity often gets ignored. As companies, organizations and societies become more global, cultural diversity becomes increasingly important.

One must first agree that there are some benefits to having mono-cultural TMTs (all coming from the same nationality and speaking the same language). Since mono-cultural teams share assumptions, world views and language, communication among team members is more efficient. This speeds up decision-making and reduces conflict. Anyone who has participated in culturally diverse teams has encountered problems on these fronts. The downside of mono-cultural teams is that creativity is lower as the potential for group think is high.

Given the challenges that cross-cultural teams face, the question becomes more nuanced and one needs to explore when they are effective. I have been privileged to serve on business school faculties which were rather diverse from a nationality perspective. This is where I spent some time reflecting on this point. My insights are through observation over the two decades I spent at these schools, which had very different approaches to TMTs.

In general, since the schools were located in the US and the UK, for the most part, the leadership was, as has been famously quipped, 'male, pale, and stale'. However, at IMD in Switzerland, it was unimaginable that the TMT would be drawn from a single nationality or language. One dean who fell into this trap lasted only a brief period. At other schools, despite the multicultural faculty, the deans were either English or American. However, I found it also depends on the leader. London Business School, under Laura Tyson as dean, embraced diversity in its leadership team. Under Andrew Likierman, not so much.

When does having a multicultural TMT make a difference? The drawbacks that cross-cultural teams suffer are compensated for only when the organization has multinational operations. In the context of multinational operations, cross-cultural teams have three crucial advantages:

1. **Greater insight into markets:** The greater the familiarity with the culture and the more steeped one is in that culture, the better the understanding of cultural consumption patterns and deeper the consumer insights. A culturally diverse team is also more likely to have superior knowledge of the political and social idiosyncrasies of different foreign

markets. A diverse TMT will also be better able to monitor changes in major markets if it has representatives from those markets, since people, no matter where they live, stay connected to their home country.

2. **Enhanced credibility with global stakeholders:** Multinational companies have to navigate the heightened expectations that global stakeholders have. They have to negotiate, mediate and communicate with important stakeholders, including government leaders, union bosses, NGOs, big local investors and media representatives. Having a diverse TMT enhances the cultural bandwidth to effectively interact with stakeholders from different countries. Making a connect between the TMT and stakeholders in a particular country is easier if there is a person from that culture on the team. With diversity, the entire TMT has greater credibility when travelling across borders.

3. **Improved morale among employees:** Multinationals have little choice but to employ locals in every country they operate in. If the TMT is culturally diverse, then it is a powerful symbol to the employees that they are working in a meritocracy. In my experience with over 200 multinationals, I have observed TMT diversity to be powerful in motivating employees.

I recall being the keynote speaker at a global leadership conference held fifteen years ago by a Norwegian multinational company. Of the 500 or so leaders gathered, a good quarter were of South Asian origin (the company had a large footprint in the Middle East, South and Southeast Asia). As I descended from the podium after my address, there was a line of about 100 people, all of South Asian heritage, waiting for me. Normally, a few people come up after a speech to exchange thoughts, but this was an unusually long line. I shook hands one by one as they complimented me. Still puzzled at the outpouring of enthusiasm, I finally got the answer when the fifteenth person greeted me. He shook my hand and said:

'Professor, I have been with this company for fifteen years. For fifteen years I have seen the Norwegians on the podium at this annual conference telling us Indians what to do. Now, at long last, there was an Indian telling the Norwegians what to do. Thank you.'

I want to end on a note of caution with respect to culturally diverse TMTs. First, as the three reasons expounded above indicate, the benefits only apply if the enterprise is multinational. For a company operating only in a single market, these advantages would become drawbacks. Second, it is critical not to assess cultural diversity by simply counting passports. More important is the international experience of the TMT members: for instance, how long they have lived in different countries, because that is what delivers some of the advantage. Third, all companies evolve in their journey to be more multinational. It begins with sales and supply chains; culturally diverse TMTs are the last stage.

Language is a large obstacle in achieving cultural diversity, which is why Chinese, German, Italian and Japanese multinationals struggle much more than their American counterparts on this count. It helps to be patient.

16

Working Across Cultures: Who Will You Save?

The previous chapter elaborated on the benefits of multicultural top management teams for a company that is operating in multiple countries. However, working with, and in, such teams is challenging. People from different cultures behave in ways we often find perplexing, and suspending judgement on these differences is difficult.

Even something as simple as what is 'efficient' is disputed in cross-cultural settings. For example, the Japanese spend a lot of time upfront in meetings getting to know one another before making any decision. In contrast, an American may see this as a waste of time and want to dive immediately into the task at hand. The Dutch I have found to be argumentative throughout meetings, but they are excellent at concluding with a resolution that is accepted by everyone.

When teaching participants drawn from a wide range of nationalities, one of my favourite exercises was a straightforward one. I would ask participants to imagine they are on a boat with their mother, spouse and child. Suddenly the boat starts sinking. None of the three can swim and you can rescue only one of them. Who would you save?

This clear-cut thought experiment revealed how people think across different cultures and diverge in their fundamental assumptions.

- Participants from the Middle East or China usually chose their mother. Their argument? 'My mother gave me life and that is irreplaceable. By comparison, I can always have another spouse or child.'
- Participants from the United States usually chose their spouse. Their reasoning: 'My spouse is my partner for life. In contrast, my mother has already had a full life, and I can always have more children.'
- Participants from India and some European countries usually chose their child, the logic being that the child represents the future and has most of his or her life ahead. They often reassured me that, in any case, the mother and spouse would also wish them to save the child.

The point here is to demonstrate that there is no 'correct' answer to the question. We must accept that there are multiple views of reality and that they are culturally influenced. When this exercise is done within a culture, the variance is small as culture can be seen as a set of rules/assumptions that nobody talks about because they are self-evident. It is only when there is a class full of participants from different regions that these differences emerge. Of course, these are averages which differ across cultures, but everyone within a culture is not homogeneous.

When we talk of cultural differences, while there is variance across countries, this does not deny that there are differences within cultures. As an analogy, when we say Americans are taller than Indians, it does not mean that every American is taller than every Indian. Rather, Americans and Indians differ, on average, in height.

Working Across Cultures

In the face of cultural differences, working in multinational teams requires:

1. Seeing differences as a source of curiosity rather than contempt. Trying to understand why others see things so differently. What in their history or environment explains this? With such an attitude, it becomes a fascinating journey of boundless discoveries and of reaching mutual understanding. On this front, I recall my daughter being two years old and as a good Indian father, I tried to get her to repeat the alphabet after me for a few minutes every day. Her Swedish mother observed this silently for a week, after which she queried what I was trying to do. To my retort I was teaching the alphabet, she remarked do you know anyone who does not know the alphabet. She thought concentrating on teaching some manners was infinitely more useful as the alphabet would be picked up sooner or later. This was so obvious, yet had never occurred to me as an Indian parent.

2. Companies that have a long history of employing people from diverse cultures tend to develop organizational norms

that supersede idiosyncratic cultural differences. These organizational norms – for instance, one conversation at a time – are expected to be followed, and are either culturally neutral or negotiated. I recall once being in a meeting involving Italian and Dutch employees. After a frustrating day, it was agreed that during the following meeting the Italians would not use their mobiles, while the Dutch promised to let lunch be arranged by the Italians. If you are in for a business meeting with the Dutch, expect a sandwich and a glass of milk for lunch. By comparison, even in the Flemish part of Belgium (as close to the Netherlands as you can get), the lunch can stretch to two hours. Yes, perplexing is the word.

3. When working across cultures, expect your assumptions to be challenged. I remember teaching sales-force management to some Swedes. I was taken aback when they argued that giving them an incentive for sales implied that they would not put in their best efforts in the absence of incentives. They thought an incentive plan meant the company did not trust them! How to motivate people differs substantially across cultures.

4. Lastly, when working in cross-cultural teams, accept some 'inefficiency' as functional. It is impossible for the team to progress as a unit without the time spent understanding one another and their differences. The 'norming' part after the 'forming' and 'storming' will take longer than with mono-cultural teams. But once this is done there will be a higher level of 'performing'. The team will be more creative as it looks at the problem and the solution from multiple lenses.

Just as we are often exhorted to work on developing our emotional intelligence, we should attempt to enhance our cultural intelligence.

17

Can Conflict Be Productive?

My early academic research focused on power, trust, and conflict in organizations, all concepts central to managing relationships and teams. Conflict emerges when one party perceives its goals, values or opinions are being thwarted by an interdependent counter party (team member or colleague in organizations, though conflict can also be across organizations with suppliers and dealers). Historically, researchers believed conflict had negative consequences and therefore should be avoided in organizations.

Task Versus Relationship Conflict

As research on conflict became more elaborate, a distinction was drawn between:

- Relationship conflict about people, values, interpersonal styles and so on.
- Task conflict about distribution of resources, procedures and best approaches to a task.

Much of the research examined the effects of these two types of conflict on team performance and team-member satisfaction.

Relationship conflict was considered to have only negative effects, both on team performance and team-member satisfaction. It distracted members from performance and produced tension in them. In contrast, task conflict, it was argued, at low levels would be positive for team performance on non-routine tasks as it helps members confront issues, forces them to take different perspectives and be creative. In its absence, teams may not realize inefficiencies exist. For routine tasks, task conflict is negative as it simply gets in the way of implementing known processes.

These conclusions were the received wisdom in mainstream organizational behaviour textbooks. And, in this view, managers should become 'orchestrators' of conflict on the right issues between the right people at the right times operating under the right ground rules. Some famous coaches were famously known to generate conflict among their team members in the hope of higher team performance. My PhD advisor, Lou Stern, taught his students that conflict can lead to growth, creativity and innovation.

While this is a good story, the results from recent meta-analysis (which summarizes known research on the topic) failed to support the above conclusions. Instead, research findings on conflict are now more nuanced, as the following:

- Relationship conflict is more destructive than task conflict for team-member satisfaction.
- Overall, relationship and task conflict are equally destructive for team performance.
- Task conflict is less detrimental (though still negative) to team performance for routine tasks as it interferes less. In complex tasks, task conflict dilutes much needed valuable cognitive resources.
- Task conflict is less detrimental (though still negative) for team performance when there is high trust between team members.

So, we can now conclude that there *may* be some positive effects of task conflict if:

- It is of moderate intensity.
- Team members come a priori with suboptimal, rather than optimal, decision alternatives.
- Team climate is high on trust and psychological safety.
- Any positive effects that emerge are limited to innovation and decision quality.

Regardless of its negative effects, conflict will occur in organizations. In the presence of conflict, a win-win approach (constructive controversy, integrative negotiation) which open-mindedly debates issues, tries to learn and incorporates other perspectives and exchanges arguments and positions to mutual benefit is preferable to pursuing a win-lose approach or impasse. However, even these integrative solutions ignore the following three costs:

- They take longer, with studies indicating it takes from 30 per cent more time to twice as much time, in contrast to reaching a compromise. Time is money under many circumstances.
- It may lead to 'parasitic integration', where two or more people reach a 'pareto-superior' decision that makes them all better off but levies costs on other stakeholders.
- Task-related and relationship conflict leads to lower team-member satisfaction. The stress it creates is related to psychosomatic complaints and feelings of burnout. Any higher team performance effects must compensate for this downside.

Given these findings, it is best to avoid conflict as managing it would tax the interpersonal and cognitive skills of even the best orchestrators. And, when it does appear, integrative solutions should be sought even if they do have some costs because they are superior to the alternative of having conflict poorly managed in organizations.

Conflict, Competition and Collaboration

Furthermore, often the conflict is a result of competition spinning out of control. It is, therefore, important to distinguish between the two. Competition is when two parties seek to 'win' without impeding the other. Think of the 100 metres dash, where the individuals run in designated lanes, or golf. The trophy is held by a third party. Conflict is where to 'win', the party must overcome the counter party, who stands in the way. Most team sports and boxing fall within this realm. Unlike conflict, competition in organizations has many positive benefits, provided we don't start seeing the competing party as an enemy to be overcome.

Competition in organizations must also not obstruct collaboration, which is joint striving by parties towards a common goal. Much of the incentive system design in organizations is focused on how to balance the need for individual performance via some level of competition between colleagues (e.g., forced ranking performance evaluation systems) versus the necessity for collaboration between these same individuals.

Amazon has received a lot of bad press for having an intensely competitive culture. Recognizing that while performance measurement systems that rank employees against each other are powerful in motivating people, it comes at the cost of collaboration, companies such as Microsoft have abandoned them.

There is a need to balance the relative importance of competition versus collaboration, with the level of task interdependence (see chapter 13: Is there too much talent in the team?). If the work environment is characterized by high interdependence, then collaboration rather than competition must be encouraged. And, the compensation system must be aligned. On the other hand, if there is low task interdependence, then competitive evaluation and motivation systems that focus on individual performance are most appropriate. Similarly, in recruitment, one needs to be aware that there are individuals who thrive in individual-focused competitive environments whilst others prefer team-oriented collaborative ones.

18

Must Power Corrupt?

Power of 'A' over 'B' is related to the dependence of B on A. This dependence happens because A controls some resources, such as rewards, punishments, or expertise, that can be bestowed on B, and B does not have attractive alternatives to A. My early research career was devoted to investigating power and I was following a rich literature in this area. Much of the research was related to the effects of power on individuals, while I focused on effects of power in relationships. Power and its use is rampant in organizations. Much of organizational behaviour that I observed was motivated by a desire to obtain power, and from a fear of losing it.

How Power Affects Individuals

As they are climbing the organizational ladder and attempting to gain power in organizations, executives need to be aware and pay attention to the emotions and concerns of others. However, the irony is that once they acquire power, people tend to lose this ability for empathy. Both experimental manipulations as well as more recent brain scans demonstrate the empathy deficit suffered by powerful people.

People in power pay more attention to their goals and are less able to 'read the room'. It seems to impair the capacity for 'other perspective taking' and social attention. Powerful people are more likely to speak first, interrupt others, all the way to the mundane act of being more likely to take the last biscuit from a plate in a room. When asked to judge their own and the heights of others, powerful people overestimate their own height and perceive others to be shorter than they really are.

Whatever we think of how desirable or undesirable this lack of empathy is, it is rational. When trying to obtain power, one is dependent on others for resources, so one needs to be acutely conscious of the feelings and reactions of others. Once having obtained power, one is less dependent on others and more focused on the goals to be achieved. The positive side of this is that powerful people are less easily distracted when pursuing a task or goal.

Power seems to have many beneficial effects for the holder. People in power enjoy better health and longevity. They have higher self-esteem and self-satisfaction. It is, therefore, not surprising that power holders are more confident and more optimistic. However, they also make more decisions based on gut feel. And, when thwarted from their aims, powerful people can become more frustrated, depressed and angry.

Power is not only bestowed but also flows from the acquiescence of the followers. Men who were not judged to be attractive earlier are rated as more attractive after they assume positions of power. While this effect may seem contrived, it is symptomatic. It was amusing to observe how subordinates start mimicking the phrases, tastes and even body language of their superiors. Given this increased adulation, at a deeper level, power changes the person's self-evaluation. It makes them more susceptible to flattery, which can feed feelings of being all-knowing and all-powerful. This is when it enters the danger zone. At the extreme, power can lead to the hubris syndrome.

The Hubris Syndrome

The hubris syndrome has been defined as 'a disorder of the possession of power, particularly power which has been associated with overwhelming success, held for a period of years and with minimal constraint on the leader'.[1] From a longer list, reproduced here are four symptoms that I have frequently observed in such leaders:

- A tendency to speak in the third person or use the royal 'we'.
- A tendency to allow their 'broad vision', about the moral rectitude of a proposed course, to obviate the need to consider practicality, cost or outcomes.
- A tendency for the individual to regard his/her interests as identical to those of the nation or organization.
- A belief that rather than being accountable to the mundane court of colleagues or public opinion, the court to which they will answer to is History or God, and in which they will be vindicated.

---

1. David Owen and Jonathan Davidson (2009), 'Hubris Syndrome: An acquired personality disorder? A study of US presidents and UK prime ministers over the last 100 years,' *Brain*, p.2 for the definition and p.3 for the items which have been adapted here.

I am sure the readers can recall leaders they have experienced or observed in the political domain who suffered hubris by the end of their careers. As this syndrome tends to creep gently on the individual over time, I used to observe while teaching that 'all CEOs have a sell by date'. At some stage, successful people stop listening to advice and paying the needed attention to the cues in the environment, especially as the environment changes. And the longer one is in a position of power, the more likely that changes in the industry, technology and societal expectations have altered the rules of the game. Strategies that may have been successful earlier in one's career may not be effective, or even relevant, any more.

While working in the corporate environment, I was very sensitive to signs of hubris, and more generally to how Cyrus behaved as a leader. Cyrus tended to encourage open debate and had a genuine interest in the opinions of others, including subordinates. But it was interesting to observe how people interacted with him. The CEOs who had preceded him in the group were far less deferential than those whom he had helped hire after becoming chairman. The implicit power differential was larger with the latter group. One manifestation of this could be observed by those who called him Cyrus versus chairman in meetings.

I often wondered, it will be interesting to see if Cyrus behaves similarly after ten years in his position as chairman. By then, all the CEOs will have been hired during his tenure. Furthermore, in his early years, he had to listen carefully to all opinions as he was trying to understand the vast group that he had been placed in charge of. Over the years, he would learn more and more about the different businesses and what makes them tick. Then would he still have patience and the humility to listen to and seek discordant voices? Unfortunately, we did not last long enough for me to assess this. But my point is that it is hard for long-serving leaders in powerful positions to stay balanced.

There is some evidence that suggests that if one has experienced the transient nature of power, then one is likely to be less vulnerable to the negative effects of holding power. I know this is not always practical, but one criteria for hiring people into powerful positions is whether they have experienced the loss of power previously. Alternatively, it's good if one is surrounded by, or has a few trusted advisors or colleagues who do not hesitate to disagree and share the unvarnished truth. Is there someone whispering the truth in the ear of the leader?

The problem is that it is lonely at the top. Everyone is potentially a beneficiary, which makes it difficult for powerful leaders to trust others. Genuine friends become fewer, sycophancy becomes ubiquitous and this isolation and disconnect from reality can encourage the path to hubris. While self-monitoring leaders should be able to avoid this, some long-serving leaders fall into this trap.

19

How to Disagree with the Boss

Sometimes, while teaching executives, I would claim that 'your boss works much harder than you do and is smarter than you'. Nothing riled up the class more than this, but such provocations are extremely important. The role of a professor is not to tell students 'what to think', but instead 'to make them think' and provide frameworks for 'how to think'.

After listening to their disagreements to my provocation, I would pick on an individual and ask: 'Well, if they aren't working as hard as you and are not as smart, how have they managed to become your boss? What are you missing?'

Often, this discussion led to the realization that people tend to select one aspect on which they have more expertise, knowledge, or skill, and generalize that to the capabilities needed to be the boss. But, technical skills matter less as one goes higher up the organization ladder. It is the price of admission. What matters more is the wisdom, emotional intelligence and social capital of the individual. In addition, most of us believe we are smarter, better looking and more personable than is the case. Both misjudging the criteria and overestimating our capabilities leads to the erroneous conclusion that we are smarter than our boss.

This is not to say that there aren't poor bosses. Rather, my contention is that for reasons given above, it is seldom true, and it is always better to assume it is not. If, by chance, one does have an unworthy superior, it can be used as an opportunity to learn from their weaknesses. Learn fast, because they are not going to last in their position. In the long run, rationality prevails and cream rises to the top.

Hierarchy in India

Now there is a big difference between having a healthy respect for the superior to having an unhealthy slavish mentality. Returning to India after thirty years, I was taken aback by how hierarchical managerial structures were there. You could see this in how people behaved in the presence of their superiors as well as the absolute power that bosses demanded and commanded. For example, it took more than a year to get everyone on my floor to use my first name.

Watching people in meetings with the chairman would have been amusing, but for the detrimental effects on the organization of this subservient behaviour. I recall going to a board meeting which was going to be chaired by Cyrus. On entering, I noticed only Cyrus was yet to arrive and most of the chairs were taken. I just headed to one in the middle of an oval table. Immediately, the CEO screamed at me that it was the chairman's chair I was sitting on. Puzzled, I asked how he knew this. It turned out that the chair in question had a back that was a couple of inches higher than the others. The hierarchy was hard wired.

After a few months, I began to see meetings as races between people trying to guess what the chairman believed, and then express it before he could. This behaviour led me to ask the chairman to hold back from revealing his stand on any matter until closer to the end of the meeting. Once his opinion was known, it effectively concluded any substantive discussion on the topic. In response, Cyrus complained that he always encouraged people to disagree. While that was true, the behaviour was ingrained over generations. And, it takes time to change the culture.

The stock advice given to British diplomats (the British are rather understated) visiting India was praise to the point that you are thinking that you are overdoing it, then double it! As one chairman of an Indian company once informed me, whether in business or in politics, sycophancy is something that is expected, and even demanded, by bosses.

How to Disagree

The challenge is to encourage people to disagree and voice their opinions. It helps divergent thinking, creativity and unveiling the best arguments on both sides of an issue. Yet, how to disagree with the boss is an art and the following are some recommendations:

1. **Disagree only if your boss is convinced that you respect him / her:** If you believe that you are smarter than the chief, it will taint how you express yourself and how it is perceived by the superior. In these conditions, I suggest don't disagree, but find another job.

2. **Disagree Selectively:** Choose when to disagree, as from the organization's perspective, everything is not worth fighting for. In addition, on some issues, if the CEO has taken a strong public stand, then it may be best to disagree only one on one, and not in front of others. There are some executives who dislike any disagreement in public forums from their underlings. However, they are open, and may even enjoy, debate in private conversations.

3. **Disagree without Undermining Authority:** It should be clear that after you have been heard and a decision is made, even if against your opinion, you are 110 per cent behind it and will work to make it a success. This means you accept that you may be wrong, and in any case, it is ultimately the boss's prerogative to make the decision.

4. **Disagree without Being Disagreeable:** Make an argument, but don't have an argument. The moment it is perceived as interpersonal, one loses the argument and the fight. To appear constructive rather than condescending, it is often better to pose the disagreement as a question. As professors, when teaching a case, we often play this trick. By asking the right question, you can get students to give the answer you seek, while making them feel it is their insight.

5. **Disagree without Personal Agenda:** The intent of any disagreement with one's superior must be in service of the organization. It cannot be self-serving, as once that is transparent, it reduces you to a joke. Disagree only after the problem is thoroughly understood, and if possible, with an alternative solution that can be logically defended as being better for the business.

On the other hand, there are situations that demand we throw away my recommendations and instead voice our disagreement immediately. In the airline industry, it has been documented that hesitation on the part of co-pilots to disagree with captains is the reason why more airplane crashes happen when the captains are at the controls.

Disagreement Is Essential

While this chapter takes the perspective of the underling, it must also be recognized by bosses that no one has a monopoly on good ideas. Disagreements are more likely to be encouraged when one views being the superior as a responsibility, not a right. Too often I have observed that bosses forget that they are leaders and not dictators, they are running a team, not a court and they have hired individuals who have different expertise which any single person cannot possess.

Of course, problems differ in fuzziness. The fuzzier the problem and unknown the answer is, the more value disagreement adds. Such is the case with strategy making. Unfortunately, strategy is often seen as a document rather than a conversation between the CEO, the board and top executives. It is through these conversations that a joint view is developed on what the opportunities and threats as well as the firm's advantage and competitive set are. Strategy is the outcome of these conversations, with a consensus on where the firm should be heading and how to get there. However, strategy is continuously evolving as the future unfolds in unpredictable ways. It should be apparent that without encouraging active disagreement and debate, the thoughtfulness behind any strategy will be shallow.

Section 4

Managing Customers

As an economic institution, business exists to make profits. These profits are generated through selling products and services that satisfy customers. Not surprisingly, the definition of marketing most frequently used is 'satisfying the customer at a profit'. One without the other is relatively easy, but is not sustainable in the long run.

In their quest to maximize profits, businesses attempt to understand both the economic and psychological drivers of consumer behaviour. While companies often focus on the economic aspects of consumer decision making, it is the psychological dimensions that make marketing exciting. Consumers too often behave in ways that are 'irrational' from an economic perspective.

Companies that understand the psychological quirks of consumer behaviour can increase their profits while making consumers happier. Counter-intuitive insights from consumer psychology are often the bedrock of brand and marketing tactics, such as making products worse, restricting choice, not seeking to be universally loved, and segmenting complainers for differential response.

20
Why Make Things Worse?

To thrive in competitive marketplaces, companies are on a relentless quest to improve their products and services. There is nothing that cannot be improved. But there are times when firms need to expend effort in attempting to make their products worse. This counterintuitive insight refers to a practice known as 'versioning'. It requires businesses to concentrate not only on making their products better, but also on making products worse!

To develop this argument, I will use a demand curve. However, one does not need to get lost in the technicalities. Even if you skip this and the next paragraph, you can still follow the argument. The simple downward sloping demand curve in figure 01 illustrates that as price goes down the quantity sold will go up. As a result, a rational marketer with a single product would price 'P*' – all other things being equal – where the shaded box is the largest (total revenues).

This leaves the marketer with two problems. First, some consumers were willing to pay more, but because one cannot charge different prices for the same product, this consumer surplus was lost to the business. Second, at price P*, some consumers who were willing to buy the product at a price lower than P* but above the marginal cost of the marketer – assume zero – were also lost. This is referred to as deadweight loss. There are several strategies, such as price discrimination, available to a firm to capture some of the lost revenues. Here I will expand on versioning.

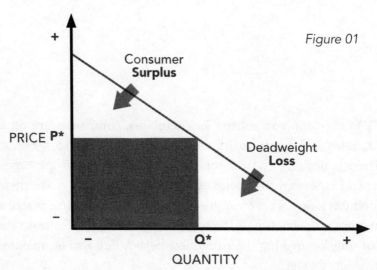

Figure 01

With one version of a product, since the marketer can reasonably set only a single price for it, one fails to capture additional revenues from customers who are willing to pay more than P* but now shell out a lower amount, as well as from customers who are willing to pay less but do not make the purchase since the set price for P* is too high for them.

To solve this problem, just as companies expend effort trying to make products better, they should direct some thought to making products worse. By having three versions of the product, the prices can be set as in figure 02, with the consequence that the total revenues of the company increase. Of course, some of you are thinking that by having even more than three versions of the product, one could further reduce consumer surplus and deadweight loss. However, before setting down that path one must consider the cost of making different versions, the complexity of operations and the resulting customer confusion.

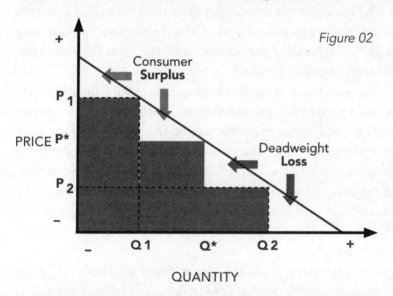

Figure 02

Extremeness Aversion

Beyond economic theory, an additional factor supporting three versions is consumer psychology. In a famous experiment, when customers were asked to choose between two versions of a microwave, priced at $109.99 and $179.99, 55 per cent of them chose the cheaper one, while the remaining 45 per cent opted for the one priced at $179.99. When the experimenters added a third version, at $199.99, 60 per cent of consumers chose the $179.99 version.

Extremeness aversion is what drives such behaviour: people dislike selecting extreme options, instead preferring compromise. That's why Starbucks or McDonalds offers a choice between small, medium and large. Given a choice between small and large, the majority of consumers will choose small. But with three versions, 70 per cent of consumers (on average) choose the middle option.

The reason to have the high priced third version in the set is to get more consumers to select the version that the company really wants to sell – the middle one. Who cares if no one buys the highest priced version?

There are many examples of companies making their products worse to extract a premium from consumers for the better version. And, sometimes, the version that is 'worse' costs more to manufacture than the superior variety. A printer company made a fast printer and subsequently added a chip to slow the product down in order to have a worse version. Similarly, Hewlett-Packard devoted R&D resources to developing the wait cycle on their printers so that they could charge more for the faster ones.

An interesting anecdote comes from a famous company manufacturing disposable contact lenses. Realizing the power of having three versions, they came up with one-day, one-week, and one-month disposable lenses. The one-day and one-week lenses were identical, save for the marketing and branding. A consumer in the United States sued the company, which got away by the defence that the one-day lens lasting for one week is hardly a breach. How can an enterprise be sued for putting in too much quality?

Versioning is typically a strategy that applies when companies are trying to deepen their penetration into the market. As such, for radical new products, or even new products in general, one will initially develop a single version until the market demand is known and substantial. However, interestingly, versioning has become very popular in the digital space where the marginal costs of products and services are often zero, with most of the costs being developmental and fixed costs. Here, companies tend to have two versions initially. One is the 'free' version to help speedy adoption of the new product by the market. Then there is a 'paid' version that helps recover costs and generate profits. All of us are familiar with this pricing system in the gaming industry as well as with the ubiquitous digital applications such as gmail and dropbox. Without a free version, there would be almost no takers for the paid one in 'network' industries where the size of the network is part of the consumer-value proposition.

Conclusion

A few important lessons emerge from versioning:

- First, pricing should not be based on production costs, but rather on value to consumers.
- Second, when there is a product line one cannot price products individually. Instead, one must price the entire product line simultaneously as there are interdependencies between the products.
- Third, smart pricing requires a deep knowledge of economics as well as psychology.

21

Does Anybody
Hate You?

O nce, I was with the CEO of a major multinational telecom
company and his top team. The firm had over the previous
decade spent hundreds of millions of dollars on advertising. Yet,
to the dismay of the CEO, while brand awareness was very high
among the consumers, these same consumers were unable to
spontaneously recall what the brand stood for. Brand equity is
generally considered to be some combination of the two factors:
the number of consumers aware of the brand and the esteem in
which the brand is held by consumers.

I was following a long line of consultants who had been
engaged by the firm. My predecessors had made the usual
branding presentations with repeated references to famous
brands. Yes, you guessed it, Apple, Coca-Cola, Disney, Harley-
Davidson, Red Bull and Starbucks. The board room had been

filled with stories of how these great brands had created such emotional bonds with consumers that they ended up as tattoos on bodies. This led to a discussion of why this firm had failed to generate similar enthusiasm and love among its consumers.

The problem often is that aspiring brands wish to be universally loved. Unfortunately, universal love is neither achievable, nor desirable. Instead, great brands are loved by some and hated by others because they actually stand for something. To provoke a discussion, I stated that the test of a great brand is 'does anybody hate you?' The CEO leapt up to this challenge by screaming 'Disney!' My response was 'American sap being force fed to our vulnerable children to brain wash them and homogenize the wonderful diversity of this world. Sexist fantasy world that simply does not, and should not, exist.' In a room of Europeans, this brought immediate smiles to their faces and more than a few nods.

The CEO, being German, and used to the last word could not resist 'Mercedes-Benz.' My response: An expensive taxi, classic symbol for those nouveau riche middle-aged people who want to scream they have arrived. Would not accept one if given to me for free!

The point is that in the desire to sell to everyone, we often lose what makes for the soul of a great brand – one that stakes out a unique position, which is different from anything else that exists out there. As a result, it attracts a segment of consumers, but is disliked by others. The problem with mobile telephone operators is that they deal with an intangible service which is largely similar across major players. Most consumers cannot tell the difference between Vodafone and Orange, or AT&T and Verizon in the US, beyond the colours and the logos. I suspect neither can the companies. Furthermore, it is consumed in a manner that is invisible to observers. No one can see which operator you subscribe to easily, unlike your Nike shoes. Nor does having a particular operator enhance your feelings of self as cosmetics do. No wonder, consumers love and hate smartphone companies but are relatively indifferent with respect to their operator. And, billions more spent on advertising is probably not going to change that.

Of course, if everyone hates the brand then it would not be able to generate enough sales. So, the challenge is to strike the right balance. As brands become larger, the need to reach greater numbers of customers makes them less edgy and dilutes their unique positioning as they try to please everyone. It is, therefore, not surprising to find such brands go into a few years of decline before they are able to reinvent themselves. Think of Burberry's being about more than checked trench coats, Starbucks being about more than coffee, or McDonald's being about more than cheap and reliable hamburgers.

The telecom company I spoke with continues to pour money into advertising, as in an undifferentiated market, share of voice determines market share. They do what they must to keep up with competition but still struggle to stand for anything. Next time you encounter a great brand, ask, does anybody hate them?

Personal Branding

The argument conceptualized for brands also applies to people. If a person is universally loved, one should be suspicious. Have they ever taken a stand? Have they ever fought for an unpopular or inconvenient cause? Has this been achieved because of their desire to please everyone and be ingratiating? My antenna is up when I encounter such a person and I am wary of trusting them. And, I now also have an answer to the question I have often faced: Why do people have such extreme reactions to me?

If done brilliantly, you can even get those who hate the brand to pay. Consider an old story of the late Muhammad Ali entering the arena for a fight. The audience immediately started booing. An observer asked Ali how it felt to have all these people there who just wanted to see him lose. He smiled and noted, 'Yes, but they still paid to come and see me fight.' Muhammad Ali was a great brand.

Nothing I have said above argues that brands and people seek to be hated. But, to be a brand, one must 'stand' for something. This is rooted in a unique view of the world or the industry, and not from a desire to please everybody. Great brands are polarizing. This is what makes them stand out. They may or may not be for everybody, but that is all right. People remember strong emotions, good or bad. If one does not generate emotion, then it is hard to be recalled, and by definition, impossible to be a great brand.

Finding a USP

Finally, a story on the importance of having a unique selling proposition (USP) for a brand. Once at a dinner in Mumbai, I was seated between Nick Clegg, then deputy prime minister of the UK and leader of the Liberal Democrats, who were in coalition government with the Conservatives, and Adi Godrej on a small dinner table. On the other side of Nick was a gentleman whom I did not recognize but Nick was in frequent conversation with. At some stage, Nick turned to me:

Nick: What do you do?
NK: I advise companies about marketing and strategy.
Nick: (puzzled look) Huh.

NK: For example, one of my teachings is: 'be distinct, or be extinct'. It's your Liberal Democrat problem.

Nick: (thoughtful look and a pause) Yes, but how do we show that we are distinct?

NK: You disagree with David Cameron.

Nick: But I do that all the time.

NK: May be, but I have not heard of it. You need to pick a big, public fight with him.

Nick: Next time you are in London, drop by and have a coffee with me.

Well, I never followed up, but the Liberal Democrats had lost their USP and were annihilated in the subsequent election. There was no reason for anyone to vote for them. The value proposition must be 'relevant' (value proposition to be aligned to the needs of target customer), 'credible' (something in the value network that delivers the value proposition must make the firm's ability to deliver it better than others), 'differentiated' (from competition), and 'perceived'.

After observing Nick call the person on the other side 'Sachin' several times, I figured this must be the cricketer, Sachin Tendulkar, who everyone in India talks about. The fact that I did not recognize him by face reaffirms that no matter how powerful a USP is, it is not relevant for everyone or perceived by all.

22

Can Quality Drive Brand Perception?

On joining the Tata group, I observed that the brand perception of 'Tata' was limiting. It was viewed as an old, trusted brand, but not connecting with the new aspirational India. Once I described it as a grandfather. Yes, we trust our grandparents to have our best interests at heart, but we are not sure their advice is particularly useful or relevant for our life.

In the context of Tata Motors, Cyrus was grappling with the feedback that the Tata brand was hindering sales of passenger vehicles. The existing models were viewed as unreliable and more appropriate as taxis or in fleets. The young or ambitious Indian consumers who desired a car to help project an upscale image expressed low propensity to buy a Tata car. Within the company, this brand image was viewed as a barrier to launching more upscale vehicles in the future.

In his curiosity to learn more about branding and marketing, Cyrus invited the leaders of WPP, the multinational advertising and public relations firm, to spend two days with the members of the GEC. Sir Martin Sorrell, the CEO, joined us for the second day. Being a loyal member of the team, I agreed to be there for two days and kept mostly quiet while WPP pitched and lectured, rather than involve us in a discussion on branding.

At some stage, Cyrus brought up the Tata Motors problem of whether a new brand or sub-brand was necessary as the company launched new upscale models priced at two and three times the current vehicle prices. The WPP team's response was, as it was during the entire two days for any query by Cyrus, that it was an interesting and difficult question that required further study. By the end, after observing all his questions and comments considered 'interesting' and 'excellent', I could not help quipping, 'Cyrus, either you are the most knowledgeable person about branding in the room, or something else is happening here.' However, this was one time I took on the responsibility of answering his query directly based on my book *Brand Breakout*.[1] I knew that the Tata Motors image problem was a dilemma that he needed to resolve.

Driving Brand Perceptions

In Figure 1, product categories are arrayed vis-á-vis the relationship between product quality and brand reputation. On one end, you have product categories in which objective product quality primarily drives brand perceptions. At the opposite

---

1. Nirmalya Kumar and Jan-Benedict Steenkamp (2013), *Brand Breakout: How Emerging Market Brands Will Go Global* (Palgrave Macmillian).

end, there are product categories in which the brand reputation primarily drives product quality perceptions.

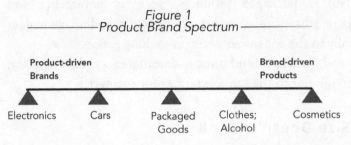

Figure 1
——————Product Brand Spectrum——————

Adapted from Brand Breakout

In electronics, the firm with the best products also tends to have the most popular and admired brand. It is an industry in which new products come fast and furious, and brand perceptions are typically driven by the innovativeness of the firm's most recent products. Therefore, no firm stays on top for long. Sony topped the lists with its Walkman and PlayStation, then Nokia and Motorola with their mobile phones, and more recently, Research in Motion with its Blackberry. Currently, Apple has the coolest and most innovative products and, not surprisingly, is also considered among the world's most valuable brands.

In contrast, cosmetics is a product category in which quality is ephemeral. Who can objectively judge whether one perfume smells better than another? And pretty much all anti-ageing creams, despite their claims, cannot stop nature's processes. In this category, cosmetic companies develop their brand promise and brand positioning first, then the product packaging and finally the product itself. It is a pure marketing game. Customers, and even experts, cannot judge product quality independent of price as they can in electronics.

Between the two extremes lie other product categories:

- Automobiles, where products are important but image plays an important secondary role.
- Consumer packaged products, such as detergents and diapers, where both product quality and brand image matter equally in the consumer decision-making process.
- Apparel, where brand image dominates product quality, although not to the same extent as for cosmetics.

One Size Doesn't Fit All

In marketing brands, one cannot usually apply the dominant logic of one category to another category that is placed on a different point of the spectrum. The best illustration of this is a story related to me by a brilliant brand manager participating in a class I was conducting about a decade ago. It was about an experience she had at Procter & Gamble (P&G) many years prior to attending my class.

P&G, tired of struggling against private labels in the consumer packaged goods space, coveted the higher margins of the beauty business. Viewing the cosmetics business as a pure marketing play, P&G believed its legendary marketing capabilities would make it a 'natural owner'. Consequently, it acquired a relatively small company based in Switzerland that manufactured and marketed premium cosmetics and perfumes. After the acquisition, a P&G brand manager was deputed to help implement P&G's world-class marketing process in the newly-acquired firm.

Despite its marketing reputation, P&G always believed in starting the marketing process with a great product (better than the competition in objective quality tests) developed through research and development. The young brand manager selected the ladies face cream category and asked for all major brands in the market to be brought to her so that she could test their objective quality. Several brands ranging from $2 to $200 were presented. The head of the acquired firm tried to gently explain to her that the beauty business does not work this way. Our brand manager went ahead with her objective quality test, and predictably, found no substantial differences.

After her story, I asked her, 'Well, given this test, you should be using the cheapest brand in the market, right?' Her response: 'No, I use the $50 one. Who knows, it may work!' As has been famously said about this business, 'In the factory, we make cosmetics; in the store, we sell hope.'

In 2015, the decade-long flirtation with the beauty business ended for P&G when it sold forty-three beauty brands, generating revenues of $5.9 billion. As CEO A.G. Lafley observed: 'We start thinking we are a beauty company and we spend all our time at the Oscars or the Grammys or the Fashion Week, which now runs for months, and we don't stay focused on the consumer.'[2]

Technology companies with a product focus (e.g., Sony, Nokia, Motorola, Blackberry, Nintendo) face the challenge of having to continuously develop the best product in the category and, as a result, find sustainable competitive advantage fleeting. However, this is not true for technology services companies. The brilliance of Lou Gerstner's strategic transformation of IBM was based on this insight. As he observed: 'Technology changes much too quickly now for any company to build a sustainable advantage on that basis alone.'[3] He moved IBM from a product

2. Jack Neff (2014), 'P&G's Lafley tells what went wrong with the beauty division and how he wants to fix it,' *Ad Age*, 20 February 2014.
3. Nirmalya Kumar (2004), *Marketing as Strategy: Understanding the CEO's Agenda for Driving Growth and Innovation* (Harvard Business Press).

to a services company. Yes, the margins and sexiness quotient are lower in the services business, but ultimately, it is more enduring.

Conclusion

This brings me back to Tata Motors, and whether it needed a new brand. My response to Cyrus was that with automobiles, over time product quality will drive brand perceptions. Tata Motors could follow the path of the Japanese brands such as Honda and Toyota as well as the Korean brands such as Hyundai and LG. All of them had transformed their brand image from cheap to aspirational for the mid-segment through continuous and sustained product quality improvements. At that time, I was new to the Tata group and Cyrus was still assessing me. He just listened, though at the end of the two days, he did tell me that I should have conducted the workshop.

More than three years later, I was with Cyrus having a casual conversation now that we were both out of the Tata group. He proudly showed me his new Tata Hexa, the people carrier on which he had spent considerable effort at the product development stage. It had been launched at a price that was more than three times higher than the prevailing popular Tata models and had attracted excellent reviews from the automobile press, with some saying it was superior to its immediate competition, the Toyota Innova.[4] Sales, from what we read in the press, were also strong.

Cyrus recalled the observation I had made at the branding workshop and said I was right that in the automobile category

---

4. Arpit Mahendra (2017), 'Tata Hexa Review: Has Tata been successful in overcoming quality issues with the Hexa?' *Financial Express*, 16 June 2017.

product quality can drive brand perceptions. Unfortunately, my three-decade experience in marketing has taught me that branding is one area that simply does not attract the best talent. With few exceptions, branding is populated by people who are neither analytically rigorous nor deeply thoughtful.

23

Is More Choice Better?

Twenty years ago, when teaching at the IMD business school in Switzerland, one of my popular assertions was: 'Instead of seeking the customer in each individual, we should seek the individual in each customer.' Today, with technologies such as the Internet of things and 3D printing, as well as with consumers taking to social media, companies have an incredible range of opportunities to customize their products and services for the individual. This enables marketers to offer greater variety to consumers.

In certain industries, customization does not have a cost penalty. It is relatively easy to customize the coffee at Starbucks or the home page of the Amazon website for each user. But even when customization is cost-effective, it must be smart.

One should not simply overwhelm consumers by offering them infinite options.

There is the presumption that increasing the choice for consumers – which would allow them to select exactly what is most appropriate – is preferable. I mean, who could be against more choice?

From an economics perspective, more choice leads to utility maximization through better preference matching. If sellers are evenly distributed along the circumference of a circular product space, then removing a subset of these choices will increase the average travel cost for consumers.

Psychology demonstrates that people prefer making their own choices rather than having them externally determined. The ability to choose leads to feelings of control over one's fate, instead of the helplessness felt when someone else chooses for you.

The Tyranny of Choice

Yet there is a stream of research, pursued over the past decade by my ex-colleagues from London Business School, Simona Botti and Sheena Iyengar, that demonstrates why more choice is not always positive. In fact, while consumers express a preference for greater choice, several experiments reveal that when complexity is high or decisions need to be made under time pressure, too much choice can be paralysing.

Consider, for example, an experiment conducted in a supermarket where researchers set up two different tasting booths. One had twenty-four flavours of jam whilst the other had just six. About 60 per cent of shoppers stopped at the booth with twenty-four flavours to get a taste; only 40 per cent of the shoppers stopped by the booth that had six flavours. So far so good for the benefits of greater choice. But the purchase behaviour paints a different picture. Only 3 per cent of those who stopped by the twenty-four-flavour booth bought a jam. In contrast, 30 per cent of those stopping at the six-flavour booth purchased the jam.

Repeatedly, experiments have demonstrated that despite an expressed preference for more choice, consumers are less likely to make a choice when faced with a high number of options. And when they do choose, they have less confidence that they have made the right decision. Given more options, consumers are also less satisfied with their choice (even when this led to better objective outcomes).

There are three reasons for the negative effects of choice: information overload, consumers not having well-developed preferences and negative emotions.

When too many choices are offered, consumers use a two-stage process to make a decision. First, they use non-compensatory screens or heuristics to bring the number of alternatives down to a manageable number. Then they employ a multi-attribute model to make a final choice. Often, when the wrong non-compensatory attribute – one that is not important or is negatively correlated with other important attributes – is used, the process ends up eliminating valuable alternatives.

The solution to information overload is to add an extra option only if the importance of the attribute is high and if the attribute helps maximize differential attractiveness. Alternatively, to reduce the cognitive effort, deploy decision-support systems that help consumers make choices.

Second, when consumers do not hold stable or well-ordered preferences, choice leads to cognitive conflict. Hence, they avoid making choices, or feel dissatisfied when they do make one.

The solution to unclear preferences is to add a default 'best' option and give consumers the ability to opt out. Or one can provide opportunities to practise and develop a better understanding of one's own preferences. Take, for example, the decision builder, which allows consumers to learn the impact of different savings and investment choices on their retirement incomes.

Negative emotions arise when all the choices are associated with unpleasant outcomes, or if they require a tradeoff between valued attributes such as safety and environmental friendliness.

If all the alternatives lead to an unpleasant outcome, consumers prefer delegating decisions to an expert (perceived as more knowledgeable than consumers) and one who is trustworthy (seen as acting in the consumer's best interest). The challenge here is for the company to build a reputation as a trustworthy advisor.

Conclusion

I consume hundreds of categories and brands in a month. Like many consumers, I prefer companies who make things that fit my needs, but also make life easy for me. If when selecting a new brand to consume or a new product category to participate in, I have to evaluate many options every single time, staying with the current brand or simply not buying is the optimal way to go.

In any case, providing a lot of explicit choices means abdicating responsibility in a data-intensive world. Amazon does not show its entire inventory to a consumer, or even its highest-margin products to a visitor. Instead, it uses a 'recommendation engine' to showcase the items with the highest likelihood of purchase for that shopper. This recommendation engine and its continuous improvement – which allows Amazon to know consumer preferences, often even better than the consumer may know them herself – is the company's competitive advantage. The benefit is that the consumer gets a smaller set of 'smart' choices, optimized for her, rather than Amazon's entire overwhelming inventory to choose from. This helps the consumer buy.

24

Should We Let People Cheat?

In a widely reported study that tracked people in Pittsburgh on a weight-loss programme, half the participants were randomly given a fitness tracker, while the other half were asked to record their habits on a website every night. The surprising result was that over a period of two years, the group with fitness trackers lost eight pounds (about three and half kilograms) on average while the group without the monitors lost thirteen pounds (around six kilograms).

In attempting to achieve difficult, long-term goals, such as saving money for retirement or losing weight, most people set short-term, intermediate goals. These goals could include saving a certain amount of money each year or going to the gym every day of the week. When these people fail with their short-term objectives, they abandon their long-term objectives, much to their and society's detriment.

Combining Ambitious Goals with Emergency Reserves

Marissa Sharif with Suzanne Shu investigated the problem marketers face in designing programmes that require considerable discipline on the part of consumers such as weight loss, fitness, or saving money.[1] In helping consumers reach their goals, marketers must grapple with the dual challenge of making the programme attractive enough to encourage sales (consumers signing up) while also motivating consumers to stay with the programme long enough to reach their goals. If the goal is too easy, consumers will not find it attractive. If the goal is too hard, then they will drop out of the programme with detrimental impact on consumer satisfaction and referrals.

In their research they found, intriguingly, that people prefer goals that give them some flexibility by allowing 'cheating' to similar goals that are either easy or hard. And they are more likely to persist with such limited flexibility goals.

They tested, in the laboratory and through field research, whether giving people an 'emergency reserve' – a predefined slack that could be used in an emergency – led to better results. For example, a goal with an emergency reserve could be to go to the gym seven days of the week with two emergency skip days (or 500 emergency calories in a weekly diet). Such a goal does better in terms of consumer preference and persistence than the

---

1. Marissa A. Sharif and Suzanne B. Shu (2017), 'The benefits of emergency reserves: Greater preference and persistence for goals that have slack with a cost,' *Journal of Marketing Research*, Vol. 54 (June), pp. 495–509.

easy goal of going to the gym five days a week, or the hard goal of going to the gym all seven days of the week.

Sharif's argument about why the emergency reserve goal does better than easy and hard goals lies in framing the goal in more ambitious terms (seven days a week) and the labelling of the slack (two skip days) as emergency. By having the emergency reserve, the goal becomes more attainable. In contrast, if one has the hard goal of seven days, then once she skips one day she gives up as the goal is already unattainable.

The emergency reserve goal is also superior to the easy goal of five days as it stretches the person by benchmarking against the hard goal and effectively putting a cost on using the reserve. The 'emergency reserve' labelling makes a person feel guilty about using it and, hence, he or she will resist dipping into it unless necessary.

Conclusion

This brings me back to the fitness tracker study. I think we are over-monitoring our children and employees simply because technology gives us the ability to do so. Rather than being soft or tough on them through easy and hard goals, we should cut them some slack while setting ambitious goals. It also led me to wonder if one could not use this recommendation in organizational settings such as the annual budgeting process.

One reason this research struck a chord with me is that I have repeatedly tried to go to the gym each day and failed. As a result, after some years, I adopted the goal of being in the gym for 180 days each year. Using a printout of a calendar and pen, I just make a minimal note against each day on whether I have been to the gym.

It takes all of ten seconds to do this, which led to some derision by friends who told me I should buy the Apple iWatch or a Fitbit and enter the twenty-first century. But this straightforward method of physically making a note, combined with the slack, has meant I usually hit my goal for the year. Despite a tight travel schedule and many pressing engagements, I try to get to the fifteen days for the month as early as possible during the period.

So, the message? Give people ambitious goals – but allow them to cheat a little. Oh, and cut yourself some slack, too.

25

How to Manage Customer Complaints

Unfortunately, products and services often fail to perform as advertised or as expected by consumers, which elicits responses from consumers and companies. For consumers, the question is whether to complain and how to complain in an effective manner to obtain redress. For companies, the question is how to respond to satisfy the customer, yet be cost efficient.

How to Complain as Consumers

When at the Tata group, I often received letters from strangers who had encountered a problem with one of our companies and were unable to find sufficient resolution. And, of course, friends did not hesitate to email or phone if anyone they knew had a complaint against the Tata group. My experience taught me that making a complaint is an art. Perhaps as consumers, we do not think deeply enough before complaining.

It is understandable that as a customer you are disappointed, perhaps even angry. But venting is rarely the way to get action. It may help you release your emotions, but whenever I received a letter which went beyond a page, I rarely read it. Some letters were single-spaced and three to four pages! You lose the attention of the person on the receiving end. Best to stay calm, factual, and firm. It helps to mention the positive. Something you liked about the company or product, or how long you have been a customer, or failing all of this, the esteem in which you held the company. This makes the letter appear more balanced and the company more likely to respond. Nobody wants to piss off a good customer.

The big decision to make as a complainer after a factual recounting of the failure is whether to ask for a specific resolution. This requires the aggrieved customer to think about what would be a reasonable redress. Indicating a resolution helps the busy person managing complaints make a quick decision whether to acquiesce. However, it may be that the consumer is unsure of what is reasonable and may then choose to let the company make the first offer. Regardless, going on social media should come after rather than before the complaint has been made to the company. Once you have shamed the company on social media, they are likely to be more defensive, unless you have a million followers, in which case your threat is credible.

Responding to Complaints

Customer complaint management is both an important and a sophisticated area in business management. I used to frequently cover this topic to draw the following insights:

1. **Actively solicit complaints:** Only 4–10 per cent of customers who have a complaint actually bother to lodge a complaint. Instead of complaining, it is easier to 'exit' and decide not to return. Consider, on a first visit to a restaurant when they ask 'how was everything?' If I have decided not to return, then this is a pointless conversation. Better to respond 'fine' and move on, or write a poor review on TripAdvisor if one has the time. Organizations must make it easier for customers to complain to obtain feedback that helps them improve.

2. **Remember, complainers are friends:** Following from the previous point, research indicates that people who have a problem and complain but do not get their complaint resolved are much more likely to repurchase than those customers who have a problem and do not complain (some studies indicate 50 per cent versus 7 per cent). The reason a person is complaining is that they have decided to continue to do business with the organization.

3. **Empower frontline to resolve complaints:** Complaints are usually received by the frontline staff, who happen to be the employees given the least discretion in the organization. Managers are always worried that allowing the frontline staff to resolve complaints may be expensive. Beyond the speed at which a complaint is resolved, all research indicates that frontline staff are the most frugal. The same

amount of absolute money (say giving a 200-rupee gift voucher) is a much larger sum psychologically to the poorly paid frontline staff, compared to say the CEO if he or she has to resolve it.

4. **Segment complaining customers:** No one is a bigger believer than me in processes when it comes to services and managing frontline employees. But it has to be smart processes, which in this case means segmenting complainers into the following four groups:

- *'Negotiators'* are complainers who want to be compensated for organizational transgression. Best to ask them 'how much' right away, as often what they ask for will be less than what one would have given them in any case. The remaining negotiators, one can bargain with.
- *'Quality controllers'* are complainers who want to feel and see that their suggestion has helped improve the product or service. They will be satisfied when they see changes.
- *'Reasoners'* are complainers who are puzzled and want to understand how this problem could happen. They purchased from a company they trusted and will be satisfied only by an exhaustive explanation.
- *'Victims'* are complainers who when they complain already make excuses for the firm. It is as if they almost expected this disappointment to happen because it always happens to them. They see themselves as victims and seek sympathy.

From an organizational perspective, quality controllers are the most useful because they provide specific suggestions for improvement and try to force the firm to change. Unfortunately, because companies dislike changing their processes, they are the hardest complainers to deal with. Usually, the company's processes are set up to best deal with negotiators in the face of customer complaints. However, offering compensation satisfies only the negotiators, which is one of the four segments of dissatisfied customers seeking a redress from the organization.

26

Can You Manufacture Customer Service?

In April 2017, the Internet and social media lit up with the video of the United Airlines customer service fiasco that showed a passenger being forcibly removed by the Chicago police from the aircraft after being boarded. At the last moment, United required four seats for their own pilots who needed to get to the destination, necessitating four passengers to be deplaned. So much for 'flying the friendly skies'![1]

In manufacturing, factories are run under strict process controls and products are defined by exacting specifications. Those employed at a production facility are rigorously trained on these processes and specifications, at a minimum to the extent relevant to their own job. In well-run factories, the employees will have a broader awareness of overall processes

---

1. www.bbc.co.uk/news/world-us-canada-39554421

and specifications so that they know how their tasks fit into the bigger picture.

Manufacturing Services

Customer service usually involves interactions between employees and customers (ignoring for the moment the replacement of employees with machines). Since humans are involved, it is often mistakenly believed that process and specifications have little place in customer service, unlike in manufacturing. Using the United brouhaha, I will reflect on the roles of processes versus judgement in delivering customer service.

For most frontline customer service tasks, we employ people with limited ability who are also given minimal training before deployment. Low pay and high turnover in these positions makes this inevitable. The retail sector is a classic example, where turnover rates can surpass 100 per cent annually.

Consider Walmart that employs over two million people. Given the diversity of employee backgrounds, low entry barriers, and high turnover, the challenge for any service organization is how to deliver a consistent experience on every customer interaction. In the case of Walmart, we are literally talking of millions of employee-customer interactions daily.

One of the service outcomes Walmart wishes to deliver is to 'be friendly' to customers. Clearly, every employee would interpret this differently if left to her own judgement. This is where the training process and service specifications kick in to create a consistent service experience. At Walmart, 'be friendly', as every employee knows, is the '10-foot rule'. If the customer comes within 10 feet of you, make eye contact and smile. That's it.

The 10-foot rule is simple, easy to understand, and requires minimal training for the army of employees. This is how to 'manufacture' services. The process attempts to remove judgement from those who may not have the ability or the motivation to exercise it. Furthermore, regardless of the input differences (between employees and within an employee who may be tired, sick, or in a bad mood sometimes), it attempts to get an experience consistent with the brand as designed by the organization.

Process Versus Judgement in Service

The overwhelming majority of customer service encounters can be satisfactorily resolved by designing appropriate processes, defining tight specifications and adequate training. As a result, most employees will not need to exercise their judgement, or if they do, it will be relatively seldom. In such cases, the ability to call a supervisor should be immediately available.

In the United Airlines case, the check-in desk staff were just following process. It is the process that is at fault if after boarding a passenger, they can be removed when enough volunteers do not come forward. Over time, I have noticed that the degrees of freedom given to the frontline employees at the check-in desks and gates have been severely constrained. While this does deliver, 'on average', a better level of service to customers, in exceptional circumstances, it fails.

The managers designing the process are the ones who should be held accountable for United's failure. Once a passenger is on board, unless it is a security risk, they should never be removed. Now it is for the airline to live with the consequences. And, from what I understand, the destination was a four-hour trip by car and would have cost \$400. Someone should have made this call, and commandeered a taxi for the employees. But, not the employee at the gate, as it is a judgement call beyond their mandate. A supervisor there, or available on call. There were, of course, other errors in the process such as not making the criteria for selection of passengers to deplane visibly transparent to all.

The flight attendants were just following the process, which in this case meant they received instructions to remove the passenger. We do not expect them to exercise judgement in this domain. Their training and competence is limited to calling security if the passenger refuses to comply.

Unlike gate staff and flight attendants, the job of a police officer is dealing with 'non-standard' interactions. They are expected to frequently exercise judgement to resolve idiosyncratic situations. A police officer's job, unlike that of a frontline airline or retail employee, calls for competence that is defined as beyond simply following the process. They must be evaluated by the judgement they demonstrate in defusing situations not covered by process manuals. Once it was clear that there was no security risk from the passenger, the police officers should have walked off, leaving the problem for the airline to resolve. The police's job does not include guaranteeing profits from overbooking at airlines.

CEO: Judgement Is All You Have

For me, the largest failure was on the part of the CEO of United Airlines. To become a CEO, competence is the price of entry. It is assumed that he or she is competent. What really matters is judgement. The only issues that should appear in front of the CEO for his or her decision are what remains after all processes have failed in the company and idiosyncratic situations for which no process exists.

Clearly, Oscar Munoz is not personally responsible for the service failure. But he does own the responses to the media and employees from his office. And, his first responses on both fronts showed a terrible lack of judgement. His initial response was to praise the employees for doing the right thing in an internal memo. An apology from him on behalf of the airline did not come until two days later in the face of a public relations disaster and worldwide ridicule.

What defines 'competence' differs by job, as does the relative mix between following the process and exercising judgement. Frontline staff mostly follow process. It is where companies 'manufacture' service. CEOs mostly exercise judgement, while police officers come somewhere in-between. Competence for a CEO is not defined, unlike for frontline staff, by how well he or she follows the process, but by the judgement that is exercised. The poor judgement of United's CEO had an adverse impact on the company's image and employee morale.

Section 5

Managing Marketing

In *Marketing as Strategy*, I observed that 'markets change faster than marketing'.[1] This is even more true today than when that book was written fifteen years ago. Marketing has fundamentally changed driven by digital disruption through the explosion of always-on connectivity, mobile telephony, social media, data analytics and the ubiquity of the cloud. As a result (see also chapter 12, 'Does Experience Matter?') nowhere is the obsolescence of talent greater, and the need for upgrading of capabilities more, than in the marketing function.

The transformation of marketing necessary for the digital age, populated by the likes of Amazon, Apple, Facebook, Google and Twitter, requires first and foremost unlearning on the part of experienced marketing professionals. One must accept that past assumptions and effective strategies are no longer relevant. Old routines and existing mental models associated with them must be abandoned as marketing tactics that marketers reflexively deployed in the past are currently ineffective.

---

1. Nirmalya Kumar (2004), *Marketing as Strategy: Understanding the CEO's Agenda for Driving Growth and Innovation*, Harvard Business Press.

The old marketing model where one made a few thirty-second advertisements a year and then blasted them on TV is over. This does not mean that the thirty-second ads are not relevant any more, only that marketers face a much more complex marketing landscape. What has exploded is the customer touch points, the need for quick response and creativity. The observation by Brad Jakeman of Pepsi is spot on:

> For a brand like Pepsi, it was once sufficient for us to produce four pieces of content a year – mainly TV – and we could spend about six to eight months developing that one piece of content and spend $1 million on each piece of film. Now, that four pieces has turned into 4,000; eight months has changed to eight days and eight hours; and budgets have not gone up.[2]

The challenge of making both the blockbuster TV ads and the many small social media and e-commerce personalized interventions requires ambidextrous capabilities. The traditional marketers, a.k.a. Madmen, who create amazing original content and big ideas for the traditional media, must co-exist with the nerdy specialists who work with algorithms in the digital space. It's the latter who do the personalization and omnichannel integration. And more of the marketing budgets are flowing towards them. Yet, in most companies marketing budget allocations have moved slower than consumer eyeballs to the new media.

2. Alexandra Bruell (2 May 2016), 'The ad agency of the future is coming: Are you ready?' *Ad Age.*

Companies can adopt different approaches to the challenge of managing the mix between traditional marketing and digital marketing. Some firms may simply abandon the old mass media approach and devote all their marketing resources to the digital platforms. Many of the new start-ups, especially in the digital space, follow this approach. Their CMOs (chief marketing officers) are given the responsibility for generating sales and are evaluated on strict performance metrics. The allocation to different vehicles is based heavily on data analytics and evaluation of customer response to marketing spend.

Other companies continue with traditional mass media marketing, but combine this with digital approaches. This enables them to reach the digital consumer who may have cut the cord to the television, as well as to amplify the messages placed in the traditional media. For example, even the thirty-second blockbuster advertisement on Super Bowl must subsequently be rolled out on Facebook, YouTube and Twitter. The need for data analytics to fuse whatever happens in marketing makes imperative the collaboration between the CMO and CIO (chief information officer). While the traditional part of the CMO budgets may not increase any more in mainstream incumbent companies, the budget for data analytics will increase. The data analytics capabilities must be assigned to a function, either the CIO or the CMO. Furthermore, the content that is produced for social media must be coordinated with the PR (public relations) function, which usually does not report to the CMO.

The new marketing landscape requires spending across the various channels that were previously managed by PR, CIO and CMO to be orchestrated. The three groups, each with differential and complementary capabilities, must be coordinated to maximize marketing effectiveness. But, historically, they talk very different languages within their silos. The integration could be in-house within the company, outsourced to a consultant or advertising agency, or managed by a new type of entity. It will be fascinating to see how this is resolved in different companies.

27

Is Facebook Biased?

Marketers are always trying to interrupt the media consumption of consumers with advertising messages. As consumer eyeballs and ears move from newspapers, radio, and television to online and mobile, marketers are mastering how to exploit this changing landscape populated by new players such as Facebook, Reddit and Twitter. As more people access their content and news via these platforms, the concept of 'fake news' has gathered steam.

During the 2016 US presidential election, both sides were unhappy with social media. For example, it was alleged that Facebook in its 'trending' news stories section was biased against conservative stories. Facebook immediately refuted the contention that it was biased. To understand what is happening, one needs to step back and examine the way media is increasingly consumed in the new digital vehicles. Let us use the two figures below to help us understand this point.

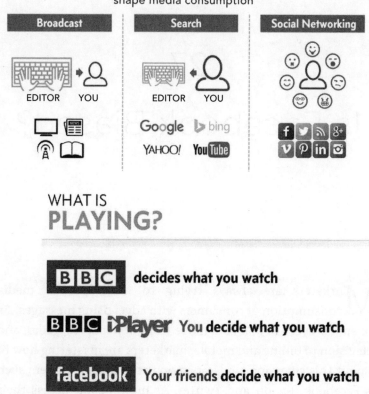

Empowering Consumers

Until two decades ago, the editors were the most powerful people in media organizations. In the face of space limitations, it was editors who decided what news would be printed, what would be broadcast when on radio and television, which books would be published, what music would be released, and what would be included in, for example, the *Encyclopedia Britannica*.

With traditional media, consumers were at the mercy of editors. The editors were the taste-makers and had a chokehold with respect to the content that was on offer.

Once content went digital, along came Google and YouTube to disrupt the traditional media model in a fundamental way. Now, the consumer was in charge of what to consume and when. It empowered the consumer at the expense of the editor. This empowerment of the consumer and democratization of control is the basis of many models that have recently captured our imagination including Spotify, Lulu, and Wikipedia.

Social media moves the game to another frame. Here, the consumer feels they are in charge, but increasingly the consumption of content is influenced or determined by their 'friends'. News, videos, and music are increasingly being consumed off Facebook, LinkedIn and Twitter feeds. What gets shown on the feed is determined by an algorithm and the posts of friends. Research demonstrates that in the USA, liberals are more likely than conservatives to 'unfriend' people based on their political views, while conservatives are less exposed to diverse viewpoints. Regardless, people are more likely to be friends with those with similar political views, which, in turn, further biases what they are exposed to. In addition, editors of traditional media now complain that much of what gets clicked on these websites or goes viral is not hard news but the fluffy stuff. As a result, we increasingly suffer from tunnel vision with the discovery portion being crowded out.

With respect to advertising and trending topics, the algorithm pushes that content which you are most likely to click as that delivers the highest revenue for the social media site. It learns your tastes over time to improve the click rate. For example, if you search for a flight to Dubrovnik, the advertisements on Facebook and Twitter seem to be mysteriously full of hotel recommendations in Dubrovnik. This is the defence that Facebook countered the claims of bias with, saying the algorithm is not biased to a political philosophy, but only to increasing the click rate. If you demonstrate a propensity to consume a certain type of fake news, more of it appears in front of your screens.

Media Consumption as a Social Experience

As social media gets more integrated with content consumption, Facebook will become a more powerful intermediary. Think of a scenario. Today, watching television is a solitary experience for most people. You come home and sit alone in front of the TV. Contrast this with my experience when television was introduced in India. I remember as a kid, one family in the building having a TV which only broadcast in the evening on a solitary black and white channel. All the twenty kids in the building gathered five minutes before the show started and crowded into the living room where the TV occupied the place of pride. The rest of the evening was great fun as consuming television content was a social experience, much to the dismay of the poor television owner. As societies become increasingly fragmented, we have lost that social aspect.

Now assume that you use Facebook or Twitter to log into a web-enabled TV. Before you decide what to watch, you get to observe how many of your friends or followers are watching which show. Would it not be much more fun to watch a show that many of your friends have switched on to and making comments which are streaming along the side of the television screen? Suddenly, you are in a virtual room filled with your friends, having an animated conversation while watching TV. Only, as of yet, you cannot share the wine and food across the internet.

While the Internet provides a very large window to the world, we can subconsciously and actively choose to either narrow or broaden what we are exposed to. Facebook, Twitter, and WhatsApp all allow us to select who to connect with, and as a result, what we are exposed to. There are as is to be expected advantages and disadvantages associated with them.

Facebook, Instagram, and Snapchat give young people a sense of identity at a time when many traditional markers of identity such as country, religion, job have lost their power. Consequently, identity has become more 'liquid'. But, one must be careful in consuming social media. Studies show that the more time a person spends on Facebook, the unhappier they are with their own life. Why? One starts comparing one's own real life with the curated life of others. We know our own situation intimately and holistically. It is unfair to compare that with the tiny sliver of life that others have chosen to share with the world.

28

Why Do CMOs Rarely Become CEOs?

Marketing professors, whenever they congregate, sooner or later start lamenting that marketing does not get adequate respect. In *Marketing as Strategy*, I presented data to demonstrate that executives who had grown up in the marketing function rarely made it to the CEO position.[1] For example, few CMOs (chief marketing officer) are promoted to the CEO position relative to COOs (chief operating officer) or CFOs (chief financial officer) being elevated to CEO. Furthermore, my data suggested that even in consumer goods companies that presumably should be placing higher value on marketing, accountants outnumbered marketers as CEOs.

---

1. Nirmalya Kumar (2004), *Marketing as Strategy: Understanding the CEO's Agenda for Driving Growth and Innovation* (Harvard Business Press).

The Lack of Respect for Marketers

The fundamental problem with the CMO is the nature of the job. They typically approach the CEO and the board for more money for the marketing budget. Usually, depending on the industry, a large proportion of this budget is for branding and advertising activities. Unlike search advertising or promotional expenditures, it is hard to directly link branding and advertising efforts to increased sales. The consequence for marketers is therefore entirely predictable:

- Marketers are viewed as having a 'spend' rather than 'make-and-save' mentality. Furthermore, in their role, they are supposed to be the customer's advocate in the firm, demanding better services, more features, and limiting price increases. All of this only feeds the narrative that they lack financial discipline, which can hardly help marketers in being considered for the role of CEO.
- Since companies cannot count on their marketing departments for results, CEOs instead turn to operations and finance to increase profitability by cutting costs or reengineering the supply chain, and mergers and acquisitions to grow revenues. Having demonstrated bottom line impact, the heads of these functions gain greater credibility, relative to their marketing colleagues, in the organization as CEO material.
- One must also concede that those entering the marketing profession often do so because they love the more creative aspects of the job. What can be more fun than engaging with the advertising agency and imagining all kinds of messages to help the consumers fall in love with the brand. It is almost a dream job, working with celebrities and models in exotic

fun locations, all on company money. Of course, I am drawing a caricature here of marketing executives to make my point.

- Typically, marketers are less proficient in finance and less enamoured by analytical approaches to expenditures. This characteristic is reinforced if, while on the job, they pride themselves as being 'right brain' (side of the brain that manages emotions, creativity) people and not 'left brain' (part of the brain that manages math skills, analytics). Any finance that they did learn during their education soon becomes obsolete through neglect. In contrast, finance and operational professionals are more fluent at speaking the shareholders' language, which helps gain credibility with the CEO and the board of directors.

An article in 2017 presented a global survey in which 80 per cent of CEOs said they were unimpressed or did not trust their CMOs.[2] The relative numbers for CIOs and CFOs was 10 per cent. No wonder the same article demonstrated that the average tenure of a CMO was shorter than for CFOs, CHROs (Chief Human Resources Officers) and CIOs. The problem is that CEOs often want their CMOs to be the champion for growth, but most of the upstream (e.g., product development, quality) and downstream (e.g., pricing, retail environment, customer experience) levers to deliver growth are usually outside their control.

Diminishing Relevance of Marketing in the Board Room

The above, especially the inability to demonstrate positive bottom line impact of marketing, means that marketing's

---

2. Kimberly A. Whitler and Neil Morgan (2017), 'The trouble with CMOs,' *Harvard Business Review*, July-August.

share of voice at the corporate level, which was never high to begin with, has declined. Research now demonstrates that at large companies, only 10 per cent of executive meeting time is devoted to marketing.

With its focus on advertising, branding, and promotion, the entire function appears tactical rather than strategic to observers. Here, as a marketer, one is talking about how to position the brand versus competitors to create meaningful differentiation. In contrast, the CFO is demonstrating how the proposed acquisition will increase shareholder value by a billion dollars (ignoring for the moment that most acquisitions fail to create value for the acquirer). Or, the COO is arguing how redesign of the supply chain that consolidates several factories spread across the world will save several hundreds of millions. It is not a fair contest.

Having served on more than a dozen boards, I observed how challenging it is for the CMO to get any face time with the board. The only issues that come before the board are strategic and bottom line oriented. This face time is critical because ultimately, while the CEO may recommend a candidate, hiring a new CEO is the board's responsibility. Compared to the COO and CFO, who are regularly presenting to the board and often included in board discussions, the CMO is a virtual stranger to the board members. Even controlling for all other factors, this alone would bias the CEO decision against the CMO.

Conclusion

What is the way out? There are several. First, marketers can become more financially driven and move into country-head or divisional-head roles from where the CEO position becomes more likely.

Second, as I previously argued, if marketers wish to be included in board-level conversations, then they need to lead organizational transformations that are strategic, cross-functional, and bottom line oriented. Digital provides this opportunity today.

Third, much of what I have observed is true only for traditional companies. In many start-up firms, especially in the digital space, the chief marketer must be quantitative and adept at using big data. They will usually have the responsibility for driving the top line and the cost of acquisition is carefully monitored. This makes such CMOs rather financially driven and accountable for return on marketing spend.

29

Why Do Marketers Fail with Analytics?

I am a big believer in the potential of big data and will use my experience in the Tata group, without revealing confidential information, to demonstrate why mature marketers fail with analytics.

Big Data at Tata

Early in my tenure at Tata, I was invited to make a presentation at NASSCOM (the apex body representing IT companies in India) on serving the connected customer. My big pitch was that 'data is the new oil'. Intrigued by it, Cyrus Mistry, asked me to explore what the Tata group should do as, notwithstanding a couple of exceptions, group companies were slow in adopting analytics.

The Group Policy & Strategy Forum periodically brought together CEOs from the group companies to discuss issues of common interest. At one of these forums, I argued that Tata touched an amazing number of Indian consumers. By some estimates almost a billion Indians consumed the many products and services provided by the group companies. No other corporate group came close.

My proposal was to launch an in-house analytics company that would help the group companies with big data and analytics to make Tata world class in this field (compared to traditional incumbent firms). The CEOs immediately saw the potential of this initiative at the corporate level. This was consistent with what I have always observed. CEOs do not need to be convinced of the value of marketing. The onus is on marketers to deliver on the promise of the function.

Realizing that the talent did not exist in-house, it was necessary to recruit a first-class professional to head this new analytics venture. To gain internal support, I ensured that the proposed candidates were interviewed by a committee of executives from the operating companies, who would be users of this service. Chandra, the current Tata chairman, who then headed TCS, was generous with his time. Together, we interviewed the finalists recommended by the committee. Out of this process, two candidates were forwarded to Cyrus for selection.

The outstanding new CEO was tasked with setting up the operation from scratch, including hiring data scientists who were in great demand. I recall Chandra advising me that this would be the constraint in scaling up successfully. Fortunately, by the time of my departure, the organization was in place.

Implementation Challenges

In discussing the challenges, I will draw from beyond the Tata experience. Please note that this chapter is related to marketers in more traditional incumbent companies, not the digital upstarts, where marketers are digital natives.

1. Many marketers, despite paying lip service to big data and analytics, are wary of analytics. Most marketers are social scientists or business majors, not engineers or physicists. As mentioned previously, they are more at home with the creative side. Managing massive amounts of data is outsourced to those statisticians who can make sense of it. It is human nature not to trust what one does not understand. In many cases, marketers, realizing that digital is the hot new thing, have relabelled themselves as digital marketers, without the competences and the motivation to use analytics to rigorously confront marketing initiatives and expenditures.

2. It was famously quipped: 'Half my marketing is wasted, but I don't know which half!' While analytics offers the ability to know more, one must not forget there was a comfort in not knowing what works and playing by 'gut feel'. Big data combined with analytics brings greater accountability to marketing expenditures. In the long run, fighting this trend is a losing battle. However, in the short run, executives can be quite dysfunctional in resisting change. An unarticulated concern was having the corporate centre manage big data and analytics instead of an outside third-party provider because the performance of marketers from operating companies would become transparent.

3. Adoption is a journey. To start, one must stitch together data from different silos within the company that are

reluctant to part with it. Completing the picture of online and offline interactions requires additional data acquisition from multiple external agencies. Furthermore, the data must be relentlessly refreshed. Without a refresh strategy, it is a wasting asset. Similarly, the analytical models are continuously upgraded and the feedback loop only works if recommendations are implemented.

Learnings

- CEOs are convinced that marketing must become more analytical and big data is a transformational opportunity.
- One must recruit for the best talent externally. Candidly, even if this is slowly changing, few firms have the required world-class analytical capability in-house.
- The fear of many traditional marketers losing power and control is a major obstacle in large companies to the adoption of big data. Yes, some marketers are enthusiastic. But, be careful in distinguishing between expressed versus real commitment to change.

As firms increasingly recognize that data analytics and intuition are partners in a dance, they seek multidimensional marketing people. It would be great if there were individuals who were as comfortable with analytics as a statistician, capable of asking the right questions as a marketer with long experience in the business, and as a change agent able to communicate the results to get action from the organization. Unfortunately, such people do not exist. Instead, the marketing leadership should have these capabilities within the team.

Data, and the ability to gain insights from it, has the potential to be a source of competitive advantage. The beauty of data is that it is what economists call a 'non-rival' good. Unlike, say, an ice-cream, consumption by one party does not preclude consumption by another. As a result, multiple group companies could use the same data. However, in a data-driven economy both the ingredients and the recipe is important. Without good ingredients, even the best recipe can only take you so far. And, without good recipes, the ingredients are wasted.

30

The Myths of Big Data

Following up on the last two chapters, this one is dedicated to big data. With statements like '*data is the new oil*', we may be at the peak of inflated expectations in the hype cycle before the sober reality sets in. Big data has now become a large industry, touted as the cure for all that ails marketing.

Yet, reflecting on just my personal experience, we have a long way to go before big data delivers on its potential. Consider a couple of examples. I log into Facebook from Lausanne in Switzerland. It is the same laptop I have been using for a couple of years to access the social site in the English language. Yet, what I see is the Facebook login page in German. Perhaps, location trumps the laptop's IP address. Still, even if it is based on location, in Lausanne, the login page should be in French. Similarly, I recently moved to Singapore Management University as a faculty member. I now see numerous advertisements to enrol in various SMU programmes! Despite its promise, we need to have realistic expectations of big data in getting us closer to the consumer.

The Myth of Big Data

The biggest myth is that there is something called big data. In reality, the construction of a useful database requires one to stitch together lots of small data from multiple sources. This is what makes it hard work.

- How many different sources can one stitch together to capture all the digital exhaust from a customer? And, what is simply escaping in the atmosphere?
- How to match data from several sources, each with its own approach to collecting, maintaining, and refreshing the data, and link it to a unique individual? Especially challenging as an individual now uses multiple devices to access data.

As one gets better at this, it allows greater integration across the different touchpoints through which customers experience the brand.

More Data Is Better

Vendors, motivated by self-interest, keep pushing the idea that the more granular the data, the better. And, of course, more data is always better. But big data is like sand grains which can create a sandstorm. It can blind you; it can disorient you. There is an old Bedouin saying that six minutes of a sandstorm is enough to make a man go mad.

- Early in one's research career, one learns that there is always too much data and not enough data simultaneously. A lot of the data that initially seems nice to have is unnecessary to solve the problem at hand. Furthermore, there is always more data one would have liked to have but is unavailable.
- Data, in itself, has no value. It is like crude oil which cannot be put directly into a vehicle. It is only a cost until it is married with analytics and refined to extract actionable information. Key decisions are what data to keep and what to ignore. Water in a glass is manageable, but in a flood, it is overwhelming.

For marketers to exploit big data, they must learn to live with ambiguity. Rather than simply seeking more and more data, the technology and understanding of how to use the data available is perhaps more important.

I recall, early in my career, being asked to be an expert witness. My first question was: am I defending the market research or attacking it? In the face of a hostile lawyer, defending market research is challenging but attacking it is easy. There is no perfect data or model; one must be able to live with the noise. For managers, the focus should be, despite the limitations of the data and model, what can one learn from it?

Real-time Data Is Better

It seems obvious that data that is updated as close to real time as possible is better. While this may be true in some cases, the accompanying 'noise' can lead to greater confusion and error. Often, instead of a quick response, it is better to take the time to reflect. Only after cleaning the data, understanding the problem, and improving the model, should one move to action.

- No matter how real-time the data is, it is past data and one is trying to predict future behaviour using it.
- For models to be useful, marketing managers should adopt lessons from the old Japanese quality movement of continuous improvement. But this requires testing of models rigorously. Before accepting a model, one must have the discipline to use hold-out samples and randomized experiments. It is too easy for marketers to adopt the spray-and-pray approach.

Conclusion

Most things in life that are important and worthwhile are difficult to do. Big data is no exception. An expert on Linkedin, in response to my comment about Facebook, added the following observation which demonstrates the challenge of stitching together the various sources of data even for a company as sophisticated as Facebook:

> *Whether Facebook presented a login page/interface to the author in German instead of French doesn't point to catastrophic failure in case of Facebook. There are several factors involved – the gateway through which the author accesses the internet and its colocation, the cookies on the system, the duplicate and differential data that Facebook is getting from his mobile activity and his laptop. The success of the recommendations/customizations that Facebook provides depends on the coverage – the author is potentially in the bottom 5% quartile.*

But the above response only reiterates that the models put into practice cannot simply be outsourced to data analysts or machine algorithms. The question to be answered within the business context one operates needs to drive what data is necessary, what sources to tap, and whether response needs to be immediate based on real-time data. Marketers are going to have to get their hands dirty and grapple with obtaining a deeper understanding of what went into the making of the model and the quality of the data that was utilized. If models based on big data become a 'black box' for marketers, it will be a continuation of the much derided 'faith based' marketing practices of the past.

31

Must Marketers Spray and Pray?

'Spray and pray is a derisive term for firing an automatic firearm towards an enemy in long bursts, without making an effort to line up each shot or burst of shots. This is especially prevalent amongst those without benefit of proper training.'

The preceding two sentences are from Wikipedia and if you are wondering whether I have decided to suddenly write about military strategy, let me reassure you that 'spray and pray' is most frequently observed in the marketing world. And, as in military strategy, it is supreme amongst marketing executives without the benefit of proper training.

With the advent of digital, and the associated companies that have emerged out of it, most prominently Facebook and Google, a marketer can have lots of valuable insight into the customer. One can know the customers' likes and dislikes, their friends, and where they are located. This information exhaust coming from the customers makes big data crucial to serving customers. It potentially allows more targeted and effective marketing communication. The problem is that the mindset of many marketers has remain unchanged from the earlier 'spray and pray' mentality despite the ability for more targeted communication.

For proper data analytics-based marketing, one needs to follow a certain discipline, where the marketer agrees to the following process:

1. Test the hypothesized model on a small sample as this helps refine the model before the campaign goes out to the larger target market.
2. When implementing the refined model on the larger population, agree to have a small hold-out sample that acts as a control group in order to assess the effectiveness of the campaign.
3. In selecting the larger population, agree to have the marketing communication only reach those prospects most likely to respond (i.e., the target market) and leave the others in the data set alone.
4. Decide how often to follow up and hit the same audience who have not yet responded to the earlier communication campaign.

The problem is that marketers hate making choices and their usual answers to the above four steps are:

• Let us not do a test as we have no time.

- We do not need a hold-out sample; instead, try to hit everyone as it will get us a few additional sales.
- We want to reach everyone that is in the database. Even if the marginal response rates are ridiculously low as we enlarge the target population, some of them will say yes.
- If we have the ability, why not keep bombarding the prospects who are yet to respond.

Beyond the lack of training and a proper appreciation that the database is a valuable asset to be judiciously used, the problem is that digital provides marketers costless communication. In earlier days, with postal mail, there were mailing costs which forced marketers to confront the cost of non-response. With email and mobile, the cost of non-response by customers is either zero or minimal in the perception of the marketer. The idea is that if one gets in front of the maximum number of people as many times as possible, the response rate is not important (these are typically less than 1 per cent). Rather, marketers feel it is important how many say yes in absolute numbers (this will always be non-zero). This explains why you get so much 'junk' email.

But there are costs of non-response from the spray-and-pray approach. Customers start opting out, which makes the database less valuable as the number of customers with active consent declines. Even if an 'unsubscribe' option is not provided by the marketer, customers start to classify the sender as a source of junk email. Beyond this, customers get very irritated and this cannot help the perception of the brand.

Conclusion

As marketing becomes more of a science and algorithmic, let us not deny that we also need poets. But many marketers will have to retool their own skills and bring greater analytic discipline to their marketing practices. The old joke that I used to deploy in my marketing classes will hopefully become less relevant. It went like this:

> 'Who goes into marketing?'
> 'Someone who realizes at some stage in their life that they have grown up with no particular skills.'

If we all reflect on the junk email we receive and the advertisements that are displayed to us when perusing Facebook, Google, or Twitter, it is obvious that there is still a lot of hit and miss in the targeting of these marketing communications. If anything, the click rates are declining rather than increasing.

This chapter reminds me of a photo shoot I attended a while ago. Every year, I need to have some photographs taken for distribution to the press as they resist re-using the old ones. Usually, the photographer takes 50-100, or even more, shots in the hope of getting a few good ones. Classic spray and pray. Five years ago a lady, who I was told happened to be the first female professor of photography in Eastern Europe, came to do the shoot. Over half an hour, she snapped only three shots. I asked her why she had taken so few. Her response was that she preferred restricting herself to a few photos she could use rather than wasting a lot of time subsequently trying to sort out which ones to use. I still continue to use two of them.

32

How to Measure Marketing Performance

Measuring marketing performance is a continuing source of frustration for companies and marketers. At one level, with digital marketing, assessing the effectiveness of marketing expenditures had become easier for budgets devoted to this domain. On the other hand, for companies that still spend on traditional marketing vehicles such as television advertising or sports sponsorships, the challenge of measuring marketing effectiveness has become more acute. Why? As digital marketing effectiveness can be tracked, unlike traditional marketing spend, it becomes harder to financially justify the expenditure on the latter.

To obtain legitimacy, marketers have rushed to quantify the effects of traditional marketing vehicles. Yet, we must avoid make-believe metrics. We can more easily measure the effects of promotions on sales and profits than those of advertisements, but that does not mean that we should rely more on promotions. Coca-Cola would not be a globally recognized brand today without a century's worth of advertising. Many years ago, Robert E. Riley of Mandarin Oriental Hotel Group noted,

> *'As managing director, I take ultimate responsibility for the brand – as any CEO must.... In every organization, ultimately the CEO must decide on the final balance between short term financial objectives and the requirement to build the brand with a long-term perspective.'*[1]

Similarly, it is a top-management decision how much to allocate to digital versus traditional advertising based on the strategic objectives and the industry context.

Assessing Marketing Health

More importantly, beyond assessing the performance of tactical marketing, one needs to assess the overall marketing health of the organization or brand. Sales and profits tell us how well the firm has performed in the past, but one must add indicators – marketing metrics like brand equity, customer satisfaction, and customer loyalty – that inform us about the company's current health and its prospects. These metrics can be more easily related to traditional marketing expenditures.

---

1. Nirmalya Kumar (2004), *Marketing as Strategy: Understanding the CEO's Agenda for Driving Growth and Innovation* (Harvard Business Press).

By building and using metrics that matter, one can clearly connect investments in marketing to the ultimate goal of satisfying customers profitably. These marketing metrics should help address important questions about the company's marketing effectiveness, such as:

- Are we servicing our customers better?
- Have we truly differentiated in a clearly visible way that matters to customers?
- Is our differentiation generating profits for us?
- Does our price premium reflect the additional value delivered to customers?
- Are we satisfying our customers better than our competitors?
- Are we exploiting market opportunities faster than others?
- Do our people understand how we create value for the customers?
- Must distributors carry our products to maintain legitimacy in the industry?

These questions will help a firm understand how well marketing is performing; they are the relevant measures for top management. Most boards of directors devote precious little time to such marketing related questions and focus instead solely on past financial performance and proposed budgets. The proposed budgets rarely materialize. I have always argued that boards should carefully review some marketing metrics such as customer satisfaction, brand equity, and customer loyalty to help bring the customer in the board room. This is why at one major European optical chain, corporate meetings used to devote a day to discussing marketing metrics after participants had presented the financial numbers and employee statistics.

Conclusion

Facebook and Google have transformed the marketing world. While it is easy to measure marketing performance on Google, my point is that we need to be careful not to spend only where we can track effectiveness easily. Instead, let us try to track marketing effectiveness even where it is more difficult by doing experiments. Otherwise I fear we will not build brands, just short-term businesses (except for Google, of course). We all need to think deeply about measuring marketing performance and it is not an assignment that can be left exclusively to the marketing function.

Section 6

Managing Strategy

Despite being a marketing professor, I was hired to head strategy for the Tata group. For some, this was a surprise. But, if one closely observed the trajectory of my writings and my consulting engagements, then the move from marketing to strategy was clearly visible. As an example, consider my *Harvard Business Review* (HBR) articles.

My first HBR article, 'the power of trust in manufacturer-retailer relationships', was about distribution channels and the focus was on functional marketing expertise.[1] The next article, 'Kill a brand, keep a customer' was on corporate marketing strategy examining how to manage brands after M&A activity.[2] 'Strategies to fight low cost rivals' in 2006 was positioned as a business unit strategy article.[3] Finally, by 2009, the

---

1. Nirmalya Kumar (1996), 'The power of trust in manufacturer-retailer relationships,' *Harvard Business Review*, November-December, 92-106.
2. Nirmalya Kumar (2003), 'Kill a brand, keep a customer,' *Harvard Business Review*, December, 86-95.
3. Nirmalya Kumar (2006), 'Strategies to fight low cost rivals,' *Harvard Business Review*, December, 104-112.

article 'How emerging giants are rewriting the rules of M&A' was firmly in the corporate strategy domain.[4]

Once at Tata, working with Cyrus, we had to answer the question 'Who are we?' Often observers mistakenly saw us as a PE (private equity) group and many believed that conglomerates do not create value. We were examining the portfolio of industries to see where we should play. Retail and the luxury industry were two on which we devoted considerable thought. Then there was the question of the relative emphasis to be placed on India versus other markets, especially China. Given that many observers saw India as the fastest growing large economy, there was an argument to leverage Tata's dominant status in the country. Still, I felt that Indian corporates did not pay adequate attention to developing a China strategy. Of course, in confronting these questions, we learnt from other firms and academics.

Finally, despite my many board memberships, from an academic perspective, I had never focused on the challenges of good corporate governance. My tenure at Tata, and more generally in India, made me cognizant that corporate governance was critical if companies aspired to be well managed from the perspective of all the shareholders. The one big learning for me from my Tata experience was a better understanding of corporate governance. This was an outcome of Cyrus constantly urging me to give governance greater thought and repeatedly explaining the many nuances of governance in a large business group, with multiple layers of corporate entities.

---

4. Nirmalya Kumar (2009), 'How emerging giants are rewriting the rules of M&A,' *Harvard Business Review*, May, 115-21.

33

How Did Private Equity Change Corporations?

Private equity (PE) makes for an easy target. Much of this is self-inflicted, thanks to the large compensation packages that PE professionals receive based on the 2-and-20 model (2 per cent management fee on assets and 20 per cent on returns over a hurdle rate) combined with the mediocre performance of many PE funds. As a result, the enormous fortunes made by PE fund managers and the preferential tax treatment of them have caused considerable derision and envy. Despite this fact, it is important to acknowledge the beneficial impact that PE has had over the past four decades on how companies are managed.

The Private Equity Approach

It is important to remember that PE is essentially in the 'repair' business. They take over companies which they believe are poorly managed. After removing them from the public eye, they turn these companies around in a relatively short period of time, usually from two to six years. After the turnaround, the company is sold at a much higher value, based on its revised performance and future prospects. The disproportional change in valuation within a tight time horizon results in a large upside for the PE fund. This opportunity exists only because many companies were not run well from profit and cash flow perspectives.

The private equity model for turnarounds in its simplest form consists of getting the right team in place and setting the appropriate metrics on which the team will be held accountable. In addition, the model identifies the strategic thrusts needed to rejuvenate the business, such as brand, pricing, or supply chain. It is only after such analysis that the team and the metrics are put in place. This ensures that appropriate talent with the required competency is hired and the right metrics to track turnaround progress are laid out. The aggressive use of debt and financial engineering has historically been a feature of private equity. Debt brought greater discipline to management. However, recently, this has fallen out of favour because of the overall tightening in liquidity.

As we are experiencing a relatively low-growth environment in the advanced world, to create value in such a sluggish setting, the focus has been on delivering single-digit sales growth and double-digit earnings jumps. Fundamentally, this is the PE model. It is what PE has uniquely brought to the table: the single-minded running of the company, not as a manager but like an owner. The unwavering attention given to profits and returns could be seen in an interview with Henry Karvis, the founder of KKR and pioneer of the PE industry. After paying the necessary homage to 'stakeholder value creation', even when discussing environmental, social and corporate governance, he reinforces 'we also saved an enormous amount of money on costs.'[1]

Private equity, essentially speaking, resolves the agency problem that arises in public corporations from the owner and manager having different incentives. Owners wish to maximize profits and managers are expected to act in the owners' (and shareholders') best interests. However, managers often do not do so especially in companies with fragmented shareholding structures. PE aggressively rewards its operating managers for the turnaround by sharing the value created on exit.

There is the perception that since firms are being dressed up for exit, the post-sale performance of the firms either as stand-alone companies or as part of another corporation will be relatively low. However, research findings are mixed on this point. Yet, after forty years of PE, if there was clear-cut under-performance, then the PE model would have collapsed by now as exits would have become impossible.

Impact on Corporations

PE's uncompromising attention to profitability has now seeped into large public corporations, especially those based in the United States. And, as an unintended consequence, compensation for chief executives has gone up dramatically.

---

1. Jason Kelly (2016), 'Henry Kravis Q&A: Worry about what you might lose on the downside,' 13 June 2016, http://www.bloomberg.com/features/2016-henry-kravis-interview/

Companies such as Coca-Cola and Pepsi have learned to live with flat, or even declining, revenues due of the tepid economic milieu and currency fluctuations. Yet they are still able to increase profits. In a recent quarter, for example, Coke's revenues were down 3 per cent while profits were up 19 per cent. This despite more being spent on advertising, which is the lifeblood of a consumer brand that sells carbonated sugar water.

Indra Nooyi, who helms Pepsi, reiterated the reality in a *Harvard Business Review* article. She observed: 'We have to do two things as a company: keep our top line growing in the mid-single digits, and grow our bottom line faster than the top line... The culture needed to change. We had to eliminate redundancies. We had to slim down to reinvest in R&D, advertising and marketing, and in new capabilities.'[2]

If you wish to be charitable, PE's effect on corporations, the improvement in returns, at least in the case of Coke and Pepsi, are coming from reducing costs that do not create value for customers. Some of the savings are kept to enhance the long-term sustainability of the business through increased investments in R&D and marketing. The remaining cash generated is for the shareholders. Of course, there is a limit to this type of performance improvement. But if companies are flabby, and many are, it is hard to argue against it.

On the other hand, if you wish to be unkind, PE is clearly heartless with its relentless spotlight on margin improvement. This leads me to end with my favourite story from this high finance world. At a party of one of these fund managers, Kurt

2. Adi Ignatius (2015), 'Thinking into strategy: An interview with Pepsico's CEO,' September 2015, https://hbr.org/2015/09/how-indra-nooyi-turned-design-thinking-into-strategy

Vonnegut and Joseph Heller are the guests. Kurt tells his friend Joseph that the host has made more money in one day than Joseph Heller has from the entire royalties of the bestseller *Catch 22*. Heller says:

'Yes, but I have something he will never have… Enough!'

34

Should the Conglomerate Discount Persist?

Conglomerates were in fashion until the 1970s, when Michael Jensen, finance professor and Nobel Prize winner, observed that they suffer from billions in unproductive capital expenditures and organizational inefficiencies. This led to the belief that companies or groups with unrelated multi-business portfolios do a lot of things badly rather than a few things well.

As a result, the 'conglomerate discount' – the value of the diversified group in developed markets is 10-15 per cent less than the sum of its parts – refers to the penalty that markets impose on diversified multi-division enterprises. Yet, Berkshire Hathaway and General Electric (GE) have been able to avoid the conglomerate discount in developed markets, and business groups are rather common in emerging markets.

I would like to distinguish between four different types of multi-business portfolios and argue that one must not necessarily be pessimistic about all of them.

1. **Type A** are holding groups like Berkshire Hathaway that 'hold' a portfolio of usually listed companies for the long term. The group centre leaves the individual companies to manage on their own without any active search for synergies between its different businesses. They see themselves as investment companies and, consequently, the headquarters have few employees (Berkshire Hathaway had fewer than thirty people at its group centre). While they can easily exit any business by simply selling their holding in it, they exit rather infrequently.

2. **Type B** are classic conglomerates like GE, in which the holding company is listed while individual businesses are unlisted. As strategy evolves, businesses are acquired or divested according to need, but in general they are in businesses they wish to 'run' over the long term. The headquarters is substantial in size and actively pursues synergies between its businesses as well as deploys common practices and policies across all units. Since the subsidiaries are wholly owned, synergies that are win-win (both cooperating units see gains) as well as win-lose (one unit gains while the other loses, albeit less than the gains of the former) are sought.

3. **Type C** are private equity firms that usually acquire companies and take them out of the market's view to 'repair' them. Both the holding company and the individual business units are unlisted. The reason to acquire is to exit at a much higher valuation within a tightly defined time horizon. The

relatively lean headquarters is populated by a few experienced executives having turnaround capabilities. These specialists are deployed to individual units and usually revert back to the private equity firm after the exit. No synergies between individual businesses are sought since they have to be ultimately shed as stand-alone enterprises.

4. **Type D** are business groups like Aditya Birla Group or Tata, which comprise an unlisted holding company and individual businesses that are usually listed. Business groups are essentially in 'build' mode since most of their businesses are incubated in-house. As is to be expected, in the process of sequentially launching new businesses, there will be a substantial failure rate here, especially as compared with the 'repair' business of private equity firms. But overall, successes will compensate for failures in well-managed business groups. In relative terms, the headquarters will be smaller than at conglomerates, but larger than at holding companies and private equity firms. Only win-win synergies should be pursued by the group centre as the rights of minority shareholders in the individually listed companies (as well as joint ventures that may be unlisted) have to be protected.

The above exposition is a result of my many discussions with INSEAD professor Phanish Puranam, a coauthor and friend. Through him, at Tata, I devoted significant effort to understanding how diversified business groups can create value (see chapter 1).

Business Group Performance

Professors Tarun Khanna and Krishna Palepu explained that the popularity and superior performance of business groups in emerging economies was a result of the poor quality of institutions (e.g., capital markets, talent markets) in these markets. This came to be known as the 'institutional voids' theory. The logical consequence of this argument was that as emerging markets matured, business groups would go out of fashion.

However, various studies since then have demonstrated that business groups continue to thrive in some well-developed markets such as Singapore and Sweden, whilst there are some emerging markets such as Pakistan and Peru where business groups perform poorly. As a result, the validity of the institutional voids theory was questioned.

Phanish and his coauthors examined the performance (on 'return on assets') of 10,500 Indian companies between 1994 and 2009.[1] Their data demonstrated:

- Overall in India, companies affiliated with business groups did not outperform companies that were not so affiliated.
- Listed companies affiliated with business groups outperformed both listed companies that were unaffiliated with business groups as well as unlisted companies affiliated with business groups.
- Over time, despite the Indian markets maturing, the performance of listed firms affiliated with business groups improved, debunking the institutional voids theory.

Listed business group companies obtain the benefits of being affiliated with the business group, combined with the scrutiny

---

1. Phanish Puranam, Raveendra Chitoor, and Prashant Kale (2015), 'Business groups in developing capital markets: Endangered or enduring?' *Strategic Management Journal*.

that comes from markets which helps reduce the many disadvantages of belonging to a business group.

The benefits that flow from being affiliated with a business group include access to internal capital, talent, technology and product markets at lower transaction costs. In addition, the heft of the business group with various stakeholders helps open doors.

Listing a business group-affiliated company protects its performance against the frequent criticisms levied against business group-affiliated firms. Market scrutiny reduces the security given to managers who do not perform, the nepotism of placing relatives in important positions, and costly group functions that do not add value to individual group enterprises.

The most telling criticism of business groups used to be the cross-subsidies involving affiliated companies. Fortunately, increased regulation in India has led to greater minority shareholder protection and related-party transactions now have to be above board. This has dramatically lowered the practice of forcing companies to buy uncompetitive inputs from other group companies, of having poorly performing companies subsidized by better ones, and of tunnelling, which refers to moving profits from companies where the business group had a lower holding to those where its shareholding was higher.

In conclusion, listed companies affiliated with business groups, at least as far as the Indian data indicates, do rather well when compared with other types of companies. And their superior performance is increasing rather than decreasing as India evolves to a more mature market-based economy.

35

Can Department Stores Survive?

There was a time when department stores were fashionable places for the cool people to hang out. I remember fondly shopping at what was then Marshall Fields on Chicago's magnificent mile. Their proposition was aspirational in cases like Bloomingdale's or Macy, and more mass in others, like Sears and J.C. Penney. Regardless, they did target a substantial segment of the population. However, the last two decades have not been kind to the department store format.

Department stores have been attacked by retailers with each of the four enduring retail propositions – the cheapest, the biggest, the nearest, and the best.

- The discount format with its cheap and cheerful formula has been led by Walmart in USA. But, more recently, the hard discounters led by Aldi, Dollar General, Family Dollar and Dollar Tree have been gaining ground.

- Category killers such as IKEA, PetSmart, and Best Buy have the biggest assortment of products for the person looking to shop within a category, especially in specialist categories which shoppers view as destination shopping.

- Traditionally, the nearest space was occupied by the convenience stores and mom and pop stores. Now, Amazon is the nearest, and if convenience is what a shopper is looking for, then it is hard to beat.

- The 'best' is the only proposition that department stores are left with, and in fact, this was always core to them. However, increasingly the leading designers like Calvin Klein or Hugo Boss are opening their own branded stores in major cities. Furthermore, specialty retailers like Sephora and Zara are increasingly competing as 'best' in the high margin categories for department stores.

Not surprisingly, the department store chains are suffering from considerable turmoil as they seek a sustainable model in the new retail world. The solutions pursued, beyond going bust or merging, are predictable.

Survival Strategies

Assortment optimization, by discriminating what categories and merchandise to flog, to protect margins in face of high location and staff costs, is clearly the initial response. Thus, for example, electronics and toys have either disappeared or seen their space dramatically reduced in department stores. These product lines cannot be sustained in the face of competition from discounters, online retailers, and category killers.

The need is to focus on high margin, unique merchandise. This has led to an explosion of private labels. While private labels do deliver margins, they rarely have the same upmarket snob appeal that comes with selling exclusive designer or luxury merchandise. Often, department stores have to complement private labels with high margin (both in absolute and percentage terms) designer merchandise.

If you can't beat them, join them is another approach taken by many US department stores as they open up outlet stores such as Bloomingdale's Outlet or Nordstrom Rack. This strategy helps them sell overruns, unsold end-of-the-season merchandise, and some dedicated lower priced lines in less expensive locations with minimum staff intensity. While this strategy can deliver additional profits, its success to a large extent is based on how successful the full-price chain stores are. That is the umbrella under which outlet stores have the cachet of being a bargain-hunter's dream. If the store can't sell on full price, this proposition is less appealing to the consumer.

Many traditional retailers are aggressively pushing online sales. Some department stores have been more successful online than others. For example, it is reported that John Lewis in UK gets 33 per cent of its sales online compared to 15 per cent for Marks & Spencer and Debenhams. While I do not have the information, it is doubtful to me that these online sales can be as profitable as the store sales unless the consumer is willing to pay the full shipping costs. I suspect for John Lewis, given that they sell a lot of white goods, this may be true. For white goods like refrigerators, the consumer is used to paying for shipping even when buying in store. As a result, they can be more readily persuaded to defray the full cost of delivery for the retailer. Regardless of profitability, only some of these online sales will be truly additional sales; the rest will cannibalize the stores. This will lower sales per square foot and the viability of the physical stores.

In the final analysis, department stores realize that the market for their format has shrunk considerably in the face of new alternatives for the shopper. A study reported that sales per square foot in 2015 for department stores in USA was $165, which was 24 per cent less than in 2006! The fact is that we need a lot fewer department stores, at least in the advanced countries. Another USA study indicated that 800 stores, or one-fifth of anchor space, needs to be shut down for the sales productivity to be acceptable.

My own feeling is department stores must do all of the above. The clearest profitable sustainable proposition for department stores that I see is for the more premium department stores such as Nordstrom in USA or Selfridges in UK, in cities which are large tourist destinations. Here, they serve as entertainment experiences, with food and wellness options. But how many such stores do we need? Many department store chains have no choice but to close their underperforming stores, and in quite dramatic numbers. For example, of the 89 El Cortes Ingles stores in Spain, one can justify perhaps 25.

Closing Stores Is Never Easy

Shutting down stores is never an easy decision. The leases are usually long term. If the store is yielding a positive cash flow, then it is hard to close them. Often the lease would have to be bought out, which means instead of a store that is cash positive, one would have to swallow a cash-negative decision. Furthermore, the corporate overhead would have to be spread over fewer stores. So the easier decision is to leave them open despite the stores being unprofitable. However, knowing that ultimately these stores will be shuttered, no investment is poured into them. This only makes them shabby with a detrimental impact on the shopper experience, sales and image.

The challenge to find a relevant and differentiated proposition for department stores will continue. There will be many opinions, but the data is clear, we need a lot fewer of them in the developed world: hope is not a strategy.

36

Is Rich Luxury Poor Business?

It has always puzzled me why people are so enamoured of the luxury business. Those who work in it are often downright snooty, which is somewhat understandable. As they hobnob with billionaires, the purveyors of luxury may feel that minions like me are undeserving of their attention.

Then there are the many students I have taught who aspired to work in the luxury business. This can perhaps be explained by the fact that these students would get to meet a 'better class' of people and impress their friends and families.

More perplexingly, the company executives I encountered as a consultant frequently spoke wistfully of moving their business into the luxury segment. I assume here, since we are talking business, and given their target market, those in the luxury industry can hardly be opposed to wealth creation as the objective. Therefore, one should examine dispassionately the attractiveness of the luxury business in the context of its potential for wealth creation.

Let me at the outset, as a provocation, reveal my cards. I have always believed that luxury as a business is a waste of time. There is no 'real' money to be made in it. What, you say!

While recognizing that gross margins in this business are very attractive, often reaching or even exceeding 80 per cent, my entire thesis is built on two arguments. First, true luxury with its premium pricing tends to have a small market. It is a niche business by definition and just not big enough for enormous value creation.

I'm not talking about Mercedes-Benz, which sells more than a million cars annually (and which I first encountered as a public taxi in Amsterdam). Apple, L'Oréal and Audi are mass premium brands of a similar kind: they target large numbers of customers while ensuring that a small percentage of their product line reaches the luxury space. The luxury brands in these product categories are Vertu, Lancome and Bentley, respectively. The ownership of the luxury and mass premium brands may be common, L'Oréal and Lancome, for example, Nokia and Vertu, or Volkswagen, which besides owning Audi also has in its stable luxury marques like Bentley, Bugatti, and Lamborghini.

Second, a relatively less important and more controllable reason is that luxury businesses usually have poor cost and operational discipline. This dissipates the high gross margins that they generate. In the name of luxury, these companies are wasteful in their business practices, sometimes even taking pride in profligacy. I say this while understanding that they need to spend oodles on marketing in order to support their premium prices.

Let's now turn to the evidence on wealth creation. To write this feature, I pulled out the list of the forty richest people in the world that Forbes compiles annually. Investigating how these forty individuals made their money or how their families made their wealth, there was no representation of luxury company owners, as far as I could observe – with one exception.

The outlier was Bernard Arnault of LVMH with his brilliant strategy of consolidating a fragmented luxury industry by acquiring luxury brands owned by traditional families. In contrast, those who created low-cost models in any given industry sphere had many more appearances, for example, Jeff Bezos of Amazon, the three Walton inheritors of Walmart, the two Albrechts of Aldi, Stefan Persson of H&M and Michael Dell. One could quibble, but the two founders of Google, Larry Page and Sergey Brin, who give away their products for free, and Amancio Ortega of Zara, who sells cheap imitations of designers, are also low-price moguls.

Moving off the top forty rich list and thinking more anecdotally of examples, let's consider how many Michelin star chefs or restaurants have become billionaires or billion-dollar businesses? None, compared to McDonalds and many other successful franchise chains that are highly prized. Similarly, in retail, the founders of Aldi, IKEA, Lidl, Migros and Walmart have all ended up among the richest people in their respective countries.

By comparison, Harrods, after nearly 200 years of existence, has a sum total of one store. That was sold in 2010 to Qatar's sovereign wealth fund and the prime minister of Qatar flew to London to close the deal. Why did he take the trouble? Was it that large a deal for the sovereign fund? No, but people love being associated with luxury, including owning it. The returns may be low and the prospects limited, but you can tell your friends – probably other billionaires – that you own Harrods. The utility or prestige deriving from 'ownership' compensates partially for the lack of adequate financial returns.

To conclude, of course there are a few billionaires in the luxury business, like Armani and Prada lower down the rich list. But in general, while the luxury business is about selling to the seriously rich, it is not going to make you seriously rich as an owner.

37

India: Demographic Bomb or Dividend?

At Tata, only 30 per cent of our total revenues were generated in India. But, we were an Indian group. Whenever Cyrus met CEOs from global multinational corporations, they always remarked that he was so fortunate to have as his domestic market a large and fast growing country. For example, between 2015 and 2030, the number of passenger automobiles sold was anticipated to increase from 2.7 to 8 million units annually, the air conditioner market to increase from $1.6 billion to $17.7 billion, while banking credit was expected to grow from 1.1 trillion rupees to 4.2 trillion.

South Asia

The growth and size of India is formidable, but most multinationals see it more broadly as part of their South Asian market. By including Bangladesh and Pakistan, two other fast-growth and large population countries, it made South Asia a must win region in the future strategy of any MNC. Unfortunately, Indian companies do not view Bangladesh and Pakistan as strategic markets. Once when I told a colleague that for Telenor, Bangladesh was the country that generated the greatest profits in absolute terms, it was greeted with disbelief.

Generally, the first foreign countries that individuals visit are the neighbouring ones. Thus, for Americans, it is Canada or Mexico; for Swedes, it is Denmark or Norway; for Saudis, it is Dubai; and for Indonesians, it is Thailand or Malaysia. Indians are different. Most Indians who have ventured to foreign countries have never visited their neighbours, perhaps with the exception of Nepal. But, they have often been to USA and UK. It is only relatively recently that Dubai and Thailand have become popular with Indian tourists.

One unfortunate consequence of this trend is the heavily biased stereotypical view Indians have of their neighbours. Only after visiting Bangladesh, Pakistan, and Sri Lanka did I experience their potential, beauty, and warmth. In this context, it is good to recall the French philosopher, Ernest Renan, who defined a nation as *'a group of people united by a mistaken view about the past and a hatred of their neighbours'*. What is so remarkable about Western Europe is how the hatred for neighbours has dissipated since the conclusion of World War II. War between these countries is now unimaginable.

Bangladesh, India, and Pakistan in one sense face a similar challenge: how to create enough jobs to absorb the large number of young people that are entering the workforce. In India, the estimate is one million a month! For those who rule India, this challenge must be taken up on a war footing. Young people are energetic and restless. They will find an outlet for these feelings, either positively, through meaningful employment, or negatively, via social unrest. As many have previously noted, the potential is for a demographic dividend or a demographic bomb in India.

Global Delivery Model

But this is not simply an India issue. It has global implications. The most important innovation of the Indian IT industry was the global delivery system.[11] This was not a product or process innovation. It was what strategy research refers to as 'management innovation' – a new way to organize the multinational corporation. Its impact is as fundamental as Ford's assembly line, P&G's brand management system, Toyota's production system, or more recently Zara's dual supply chain model.

The global services model was invented, or perhaps simultaneously developed, in the late 1990s by many Indian information technology companies. It allows for what were previously tightly integrated tasks performed by workers in one location working for a single company to now take on a distributed format. This allows for different parts of the work to be executed in different geographies and by different organizations.

The advantages are obvious. They include working wherever the best expertise exists at the lowest possible costs, taking advantage of time-zone differences for round-the-clock efforts, and diversifying risk by building redundancy across locations.

---

1. Nirmalya Kumar and Phanish Puranam (2011), *India Inside: The Emerging Innovation Challenge to the West*, Harvard Business Review Press.

Potential challenges are equally obvious: how to get people to work effectively across barriers erected by organizations, nations, cultures, and time zones.

What the global delivery system enables is to make India's young workforce globally relevant. Jobs for them are now not exclusively a function of the opportunities to serve the Indian market. While it cannot create the needed jobs to absorb the millions being added each year to India's workforce, it comes at an opportune time for many parts of the world that are facing the opposite crisis of declining birth rates.

Low Birth Rates in Developed Nations

For the moment, let us say 'women' are not having enough children in developed countries. As countries develop, the birth rate plummets as women get more educated and have greater employment opportunities outside the home.

The birth rate especially plunges in those advanced countries where higher education of women is combined with the continued prevalence of traditional sex roles. In such cultures, women quickly realize the men are not going to provide much help with childcare and their own outside employment opportunities are substantial. Among the large countries, Japan and South Korea, or for that matter even Italy and Russia, having very low fertility rates should therefore not come as any surprise.

From a global perspective, beyond the advanced nations, China with its large but declining population exacerbates this problem. Because of its historical one child policy, as the quip goes: 'China will become old before it becomes rich.'

For the countries with a declining population and a worsening ratio of working age to retired people, there are only two choices. One is to entice women to have more children, and governments are trying all sorts of creative ways to do this. However, I doubt a few thousand dollars for another child will tip the scales for any rational person.

The alternative is the politically unacceptable solution of greater immigration. Given the reality on the ground, the current attitudes toward immigration in the developed nations demonstrate how little effort has been devoted to educating the masses about this existential challenge. Instead, we observe demagoguery.

Where Does This Leave Us?

Closing the loop to India, let me reiterate that I do not believe that the global delivery system alone can solve the job creation problem of India. But, we need to see India's workforce as the world's workforce. The world must adopt them.

This does not, however, absolve India from the need to prepare its youth for employment. Nowhere in the world is primary education anything but a government-funded program. There is no business model yet invented that can 'profit' from educating all children in a nation to their fullest potential. On the supply side, India must educate its children. They are too precious to the world to neglect.

In conclusion, I hope India will work on creating jobs from the demand side by removing as many barriers as possible to employment generation. My sojourn only reinforced my belief that India is still an agonizingly difficult place to do business.

What Makes India Special?

To end on a positive note, let me reflect on one aspect that is vivid to me from the four years that I spent in India after having lived out of the country for thirty years. One of the remarkable things that strikes visitors, especially foreigners, about India is the warmth of the people one encounters. Individuals think nothing about dropping everything and going out of their way to help you without any expectation of reciprocity. They even get embarrassed if you so much as thank them for their generosity.

An intriguing aspect of this trait for the wealthier Indians is that this large-heartedness extends to their acquaintances. You are introduced to someone at a party and the next minute they will invite you into their home or agree to assist you with a problem you are facing. And, believe me, in India you are never far away from a bureaucratic hurdle that will be impossible to solve using the regular channels. There is always a shortcut around the obstacle, but it is through a 'friend' or a friend of a friend.

In the more impoverished sections of society, strangers will offer help to strangers without any expectation of ever meeting again. They will do the good deed and simply walk away before one can acknowledge it. It is generalized reciprocity at work.

This book is dedicated to those whom I met during my three and a half years working for the Tata group in India. No matter where I live, I will always fondly recall that in India, nothing is too much trouble.

38

Do You Have a China Strategy?

China is becoming so large that every multinational business must have a China strategy. This may not always mean selling in China, though that is an attractive proposition for many companies. It could include activities such as having the supply chain dip into China as well as strategies to compete against or collaborate with Chinese companies.

Given the importance of China to the Tata portfolio, Cyrus and some of the GEC members decided to spend a week exploring the country in 2015. Through the brilliant connections of my GEC ex-colleague Madhu Kannan, we met with more than thirty companies in China, usually, their founder or CEO. Of the many impressive companies, I will profile three, before observing some takeaways.

BYD: Can China Lead the Electric Car Industry?

A visit to BYD, the automaker, brought to life the aggressive changes that China is making with respect to electric vehicles. Frankly, Chinese automakers have struggled against foreign competition. After thirty years of trying to build an auto industry, all they have produced are copycat models. This has been a disappointment for the government, whose aspiration for the Chinese automobile makers has been that they become world beaters like the Japanese and Koreans.

Observing the cars, the quality had improved in recent years but it still lagged world-class standards. However, finally, the Chinese believe that they have found a lever to leapfrog competition. It is through electric vehicles. The government is giving huge subsidies to the automakers for electric vehicles – up to a million RMB per bus and INR 1,337,957 per car. This subsidy is not available to foreign makers such as Tesla. It is expected that the subsidy will be removed by 2020/2022. By then, electric vehicles should be commercially viable on a stand-alone basis.

The money spent on this subsidy is recovered through the taxes levied on luxury cars and carbon emissions. Beyond the subsidy, electric vehicles are encouraged by not having any licensing fee, nor any day of driving restrictions placed on them. Furthermore, Beijing has begun to issue only a limited number of licences for traditional fuel vehicles. As a result, 2015 saw greater sales of electric vehicles in China than all the previous years combined!

Why is the government pushing so hard? The espoused reason is national security – to reduce the dependence on oil imports. But, perhaps the other impetus is that the government is worried about the political ramifications if they do not solve the pollution problem in the cities, especially in Beijing. One wonders about the implications on demand for oil as this transformation happens.

Ping An: Employing 1 in Every 1,000 Chinese

Ping An, the leading insurer in China, has sales of approximately $106 billion, market cap of $100 billion, and profits of $9.6 billion. It employs an army of 1.3 million, of which 900,000 are the salesforce serving 80 million clients. As the founder proudly stated, 1 in a 1,000 Chinese works for them!

How does Ping An get a 900,000 person salesforce to be productive? They launched a 100-million-dollar sales training initiative which uses gamification extensively. This allows the salesforce to train themselves in their spare time and move up the proficiency levels as they become more knowledgeable. Yes, the Chinese protect their domestic companies, but out of this process they have built some great companies too. A new iconic headquarters building was just completed to reflect the fact that it is the most valuable insurance brand in the world, worth $16 billion.

DJI: Flying High with Drones

Finally, we paid a visit to DJI, which is the world leader in commercial drones, with a reported 70 per cent market share. A young kid set up this company after tinkering with drones during his university education. Two of his professors are on the board of directors.

What this, and the many other companies we visited in the digital space, demonstrated was the huge entrepreneurial energy in China. Most of the companies are less than twenty years old, many less than ten. But they dream really big and have a R&D-driven focus. For example, Huawei has a 13 per cent R&D expenditure ($9 billion a year, more than the $8 billion that Apple spends). When we visited their main R&D centre, it was a 1-kilometre-long building.

What I found had changed from my last visit to China three years before, when I was researching the *Brand Breakout* book, was the English fluency among the executives. It had vastly improved. They were also many women in leadership positions and all the top executives as well as entrepreneurs struck me as really smart people.

Conclusion

This does not mean China does not have challenges such as six years minimum inventory of residential property, a bad loan book, and a difficult transition from an infrastructure-manufacturing led growth to a consumption-service led growth. Yet, on the third day of the trip, I had an epiphany. Despite all the talk of slowdown, in China, I was seeing the future. On reflection, I realized that this understanding was a transformation of my thinking that had taken six or seven years to happen. In 2009, the following passage appeared in my book, *India's Global Powerhouses*, on page 17:

> 'These ambivalent feelings toward globalization are also seeping into popular Western culture. The 2008 French movie Summer Hours, directed by Olivier Assayas, is about a successful French couple working abroad. Assayas in an interview was nostalgic but realistic when he observed: "It is not their own logic that takes them away from home, it is the logic of the world today. If you are young and successful,

you look towards India or China . . . The world is changing
in Russia, China, India, the Middle East . . . it's like an
earthquake. They are absorbing all the energy. You don't feel
that sense of change in Europe."'

During the Beijing Olympics, the *New York Times* carried a story
about the changing architecture of the city:

'If Westerners feel dazed and confused upon exiting the
plane at the new international airport terminal here, it's
understandable. It's not just the grandeur of the space. It's
the inescapable feeling that you're passing through a portal
to another world, one whose fierce embrace of change has left
Western nations in the dust.'

The article went on to compare the sensation to the epiphany
that Adolf Loos, the Austrian architect, experienced more than
a century ago. On stepping off the boat in New York harbour,
Loos realized that he had seen the future, and Europe was now
culturally obsolete.

It's the same feeling I got in China, on this, my fifth trip there.

39

Should Business School Faculty Be Executives?

Given my vast network of faculty around the world, I was often asked for experts who could help with specific problems. Among the faculty that I managed to secure for were Marcus Alexander for strategy, Simona Botti and David Faro for branding, all from London Business School, Phanish Puranam for business groups from INSEAD, Jean-Philippe Deschamps for innovation from IMD, Rajiv Lal for retailing from Harvard, James Anderson, Greg Carpenter, and Philip Kotler for marketing from Northwestern, and Pradeep Chintagunta for big data from Chicago.

MBA students are often puzzled why faculty at top business schools are not either current or former executives with so-called 'real-world experience'. Instead, academics with PhDs teach the next generation of executives. More interestingly, the faculty that I brought in to help were more frequently teaching senior executives rather than degree students.

The overwhelming majority of faculty members have never been entrepreneurs or executives with any meaningful business experience. The higher ranked the business school is, the more likely the faculty member is someone with academic rather than real-world experience. As I am convinced of the merits of the approach followed by leading institutions, let me explain the logic.

Teaching Is Not the Main Job

In seeking an academic position, beyond compensation, the other equally important criteria in selecting which university should be home is what is called 'teaching load'. How much will I have to teach each year? Each school has a somewhat different metric – points, hours, courses, or days. Ultimately, they all boil down to how many hours of contact time with students in a year is required, and how this teaching load will be distributed across the year. Fewer total hours which can be aggregated within a short time is best, as it leaves the rest of the year free.

For example, my teaching load at London Business School could be delivered in twenty days spread across eight weeks in the year. A degree course at London Business School met twenty times for 90 minutes. Three courses were done in the week format of all-day teaching, while one course met every other weekend for a day. Of course, these contact hours do not include preparation and grading. Since I could teach the advanced marketing strategy elective in my sleep and it generated enough demand for four sections, the preparation time was inconsequential.

Grading took another week per course. However, if I taught in executive education, then there was no grading. This situation never ceased to amaze my friends, who queried what I did with the rest of my time.

The higher the university is ranked, the more the real job of the faculty member is creating new knowledge that others will teach. For example, a medical university trains budding doctors how to cure cancer. But someone has to generate the knowledge on the latest cure for cancer. The faculty at the lower-ranked schools only teach. The faculty at the top-ranked schools compete on finding the cure for cancer. And, as I always used to remark, if one is working on finding the cure to cancer, then please do not 'waste' time teaching. The faculty member is more valuable to society and the profession pursuing research. Any teaching by such faculty members is better focused by mentoring PhD students working on their teams.

I realize that the above example is extreme. But it helps make the point. Undoubtedly, no one in business schools is working on anything even remotely as important as the cure for cancer. Therefore, one should expect all business school faculty to spend at least some time in the classroom with students. In my case, the remaining time was spent on research and the efficient teaching load helped me write seven books in my ten years at London Business School. Besides the books, there were eight appearances in *Harvard Business Review* as well as many cases and academic papers. In addition, on average, one day a week was devoted to being on corporate boards and consulting as per my contract. This helped bring real-world experience into the classroom and my writing as well as make a few bucks. The point here is not to recite my vita during my stint at London Business School but to demonstrate the allocation of time by a faculty member.

Understanding Causation

Over the years, I have invited scores of executives to present in my classes. The response from the students has been overwhelmingly positive. They loved executives telling them stories from the organizations. Since I only selected executives to speak from the leading organizations, Google and Facebook were two of my favourites in recent years; these sessions are set up for success. Who would not want to know what Google or Facebook are thinking. Alternatively, I would have a dynamic speaker with a great product launch or successful turnaround story.

Yet, one must be careful with this approach. The executives were excellent at presenting their story, or 'what they did'. But, poor at articulating why the results occurred. Usually, success was attributed to apple pie and motherhood statements such as people, culture, leadership and strategy. Yet the same strategy may not be transferable to another context, company, industry or time.

In general, we are not taught to think of causation in a critical manner unless trained to do so. This is what great doctoral programmes do, regardless of the discipline. Research faculty are experts at elaborating the moderating conditions under which a particular variable is likely to lead to success or failure.

Why Are Indians in USA So Successful?

For example, there was a video making the rounds on social media which documented the remarkable success of Indians in USA.[1] The hosts explain this success via the usual tautological

---

1. https://youtube/-da_No_GBIQ

cultural explanations of Indians having better work ethic, higher emphasis on education, and greater propensity to become entrepreneurs. As an academic, I would find all these explanations unsatisfactory. If these were the reasons, then Indians everywhere would be just as successful.

In contrast, consider the recent book '*The Other One Percent: Indians in America*' (authored by Sanjoy Chakravorty, Devesh Kapur, and Nirvikar Singh and published by Oxford University Press). They reveal the 'triple selection' argument for the success of Indians in USA:

> '*First, those arriving were drawn from the upper strata of Indian society, and especially its upper castes. Second, they were products of exacting Indian academic institutions, often with skills in engineering and computer science. Finally, they were thinned out by US immigration rules, which favored clever students and skilled workers. Indian Americans have been selected to be outliers.*'

Voila! That explains why we do not see the same levels of over-performance by Indians in other countries, especially where they migrated as indentured labour.

The responsibility of faculty is to debunk widely held myths and simplistic causal inferences through research, reflection, analytical rigour, and data. This process helps develop a more nuanced and complex understanding of how the world works. It is precisely such moderated explanations that one needs as a thoughtful executive to succeed at strategy making. Only under certain specific conditions is any particular strategy likely to succeed. Typically, a single success story, no matter how inspiring, cannot reveal the moderating conditions, as there is no variance or counter-factual evidence.

40

Can You Learn from Executive War Stories?

In the previous chapter, I argued why faculty at the leading business schools in the world tend to be researchers with PhDs rather than executives. However, there are two important points that should be noted in this context.

First, I am not claiming that all schools should have research as a mission, and therefore, be populated by research faculty. In fact, except for the top 50 or 100 business schools in the world, the rest of the degree-awarding institutions would be better served by focusing on delivering a great classroom experience. The reality is that research is an elitist pursuit.

Second, teaching a semester-long course requires strong theoretical and conceptual frameworks. This does not imply that executives do not have great knowledge and experiences to share. Their 'war stories' can lead to valuable insights but only when interpreted with the help of theoretical frameworks.

The best executive stories are rather nuanced, with an elaboration of the conditions that led to success or failure. I share two such anecdotes that were told in my class around a decade ago which I have used repeatedly. When at Tata, I also thought deeply about them and how they would apply.

Acquisitions at Reckitt Benckiser

Mergers and acquisitions (M&A), as those who follow the academic literature know, are fraught with high failure rates. The usual number given is that 70 per cent of deals, on average, do not create value from the perspective of the shareholders of the acquiring company. Yet acquirers like Cisco or the more successful private equity players have demonstrated that acquisitions can be an effective strategy. Not surprisingly, as an academic, I have always sought the secret of those companies that have been serial acquirers and still created value for their shareholders.

A presenter from Reckitt Benckiser, a company that I admire, now led by my friend Rakesh Kapoor, once elaborated the acquisition strategy of the company. As a caveat, please note that this was more than a decade ago, so their acquisition strategy may have changed. He went on to say that before Reckitt acquires a company, they look for the following three conditions to be fulfilled:

1. The potential target company is in the space where the basis of competition is more on 'functional' and 'rational' criteria rather than purely 'emotional' or 'symbolic' attributes. For

whatever reason, Reckitt management believed that they had not mastered managing the latter types of businesses. Clearly, this implied a company should stick to its competences and what it knows how to manage.

2. The margins in the target company were higher than the margins at Reckitt Benckiser. This ensured that the acquisition did not dilute their overall earnings quality. As a result, applying Reckitt's pre-acquisition PE (price earnings) ratio should support a higher overall post-acquisition valuation.

3. Reckitt could see a clear path for the target company that would enhance the current growth rate of the acquired company. This meant that there was potential for Reckitt to add value to the acquired company.

For me, such an anecdote is insightful as it leads me to provoke the audience to reflect on their own acquisition strategy, considering the 70 per cent base failure rate. No wonder the operating margins at Reckitt Benckiser are almost twice those at Danone, Nestlé, or Unilever. While strategies must change over time, it remains a well-managed company with a focus on earnings.

Exits at Vodafone

The second anecdote comes from Arun Sarin, who was the former CEO of Vodafone. Presenting to a class of mine, he recounted the sale of Vodafone Japan. Vodafone was struggling in Japan when it received an offer in excess of $15 billion from Softbank for Vodafone's Japanese unit. Arun asked his chief financial officer (CFO) to run the numbers. The CFO reverted that for this valuation to be justified, Vodafone's margins had to expand by X per cent and its market share had to increase to Y per cent (I cannot recall the actual numbers or whether Arun shared those with my class). Given the almost monopoly status of DoCoMo in Japan, Arun knew neither of these two assumptions were likely to happen. As a result, he sold Vodafone Japan.

The resulting cash from the exit of Vodafone Japan was useful. A large part of it was returned to the restive shareholders who were unhappy at Vodafone's recent lacklustre performance as well as the large losses in Germany and Italy. The remaining cash helped Vodafone acquire its way into India, which was then one of the most exciting mobile telephony markets. This Indian entry did run into some well-known challenges, but that is another story.

But, Arun's story became better. Subsequent to the sale of Japan, Arun received an offer from a private equity firm for the assets of Vodafone New Zealand. Once again, the CFO was asked to run the numbers. The results were similar. The assumptions needed to justify the offer from a financial perspective were aggressive. As a result, like in the case of the Japanese unit, the net present value for Vodafone for the New Zealand business was less than the offer on the table.

This time Arun refused to sell. His logic was that the New Zealand business was one of the smallest of the forty or so countries that Vodafone operated in. The sale or retention of the New Zealand business would have no financial impact on the overall fortunes of Vodafone. However, from a management perspective, a small operation such as New Zealand or Ireland was important to have in the Vodafone portfolio.

These small countries could be viewed as laboratories for high-potential talent. By assigning people there, one could observe their performance in a low-risk environment for Vodafone. Even if they failed, it would not impact the global Vodafone results. Yet, the performance of top executives in these small countries helped evaluate and develop top management talent for future roles in larger countries.

So, the best executive stories have learnings that make our conceptual frameworks come alive. Great teachers and executives combine the two.

41

Must You Fail to Learn?

Many years ago, I shared a taxi from Singapore airport to my hotel with Chris Argyris. Chris was a business school professor, who ended his career at Harvard and unfortunately passed away in 2013. His research focused on why organizations and people find it so hard to learn. His most approachable article is 'Teaching Smart People How to Learn', published in the *Harvard Business Review*, May-June 1991.

The big point that Chris made was that business success depends on the ability to learn but most people / organizations do not know how to learn. They excel at solving problems created by external forces but they fail to recognize that to learn one needs to look inward at one's own behaviour. He distinguished between two types of learning:

- **Single loop:** A thermostat set to 68 degrees turns up the heat whenever the temperature drops below 68.
- **Double Loop:** One asks why the thermostat is set to 68 degrees. Is that the optimum temperature?

Managers have a body of knowledge, and it is, ironically, this that constrains their learning. They have a difficult time thinking outside the box and do not know how to learn from failure. When challenged, they become very defensive and tend to focus attention away from their own behaviour to that of others. Argyris called this defensive reasoning.

Professionals also go into a doom loop of despair if they don't perform perfectly or if they do not receive adequate recognition. Argyris stated that 'everyone develops a theory of action – a set of rules that individuals use to design and implement their own behaviours as well as to understand the behaviour of others'. However, people don't usually follow their stated action theories. The way they really behave can be called their theory-in-use.

Back to the taxi. Figuring that I had him captive, I asked what he had found in his research that is most useful for managers. He said that most dysfunctionalities that one observed in organizations were driven by managers who (theories in use):

1. want to have unilateral control, especially over all the resources they need
2. love to 'win' and so act to maximize 'winning' and minimize 'losing'
3. hate to lose face and suppress negative feelings
4. wish to appear as 'rational' as possible.

I have to confess that this stuck in my head forever. Yet, at that time, I did not realize how insightful it was. While in the corporate world as an executive, I often smiled to myself when I recognized behaviour (my own included) that was being driven by these four factors, and the resulting negative consequences for the firm.

But let us not lose all hope. Chris believed that people could be taught to 'identify the inconsistencies between their espoused and actual theories of action'. To do so, they need to learn to use the same strategies that effective organizations use: collect valid data, analyse it, and constantly test the inferences drawn from the data. Organizations can help by starting with top-down change. Top-level managers must first learn to change their defensive behaviour before we can see broader change across the organization.

Learning from Failures

It is common to hear that 'we celebrate failures in our organization' – I assume this means we learn from failures. My belief has always been that failures are acceptable, provided:

1. You don't bet the company.
2. You don't make the same mistake twice.
3. You learn something useful for yourself and the organization.

The first two are relatively straightforward so I will elaborate only on the third. In any post-mortem, it is always helpful to ask: could this mistake have been prevented? If due diligence by an individual or an organization unit would have led not to attempt the action that led to failure, then one starts to question the judgement of the actor(s). However, post hoc, it is always easy to see how something could have been prevented.

A useful practice to improve major decisions is to conduct what is called a pre-mortem. Here team members, at the start of a project, engage in a thought experiment. They assume that the project has failed in the future. Then based on this assumption, team members generate the potential reasons why the project failed. The causes that are elicited are then utilized to strengthen the proposed plan.

In a corporate environment, one challenge is to evaluate the decision not by the outcome, but by the judgement displayed at the time of the decision. The latter is very hard to do. Too frequently, meetings where major decisions were made would conclude by someone saying we will find out how good this decision is when the results come in. But the success or failure of any future action depends on many external factors that are unknown at present. All one can do at the time of making the decision is to ensure making the best decision in light of the facts available at that particular moment.

Before attributing a mistake as a failure of judgement on the part of the actor, one must have repeated observations of the actor. If a person repeatedly makes similar mistakes, then they are failing to learn. Here we must distinguish between experience and learning. Two people with similar experience may have very different learning capabilities. Experience is more valuable when the person has thought deeply about what led to success and failure.

Attributing the causes of success and failure is susceptible to the well-known fundamental attribution bias. We tend to attribute our success to internal factors such as our ability and hard work. But, when it comes to our failures, we tend to attribute it to external circumstances or bad luck. In contrast, our attributions for the success and failures of others runs in the opposite direction.

One may argue that learning can only occur through failure. If one succeeds, then either the answer was known or there was a theory that could predict the solution. To learn, one must try things that are beyond one's competence and knowledge. And, this will result in failures. A learning oriented person fails often, but does not make the same mistake twice. And, it is through such failures that we build long-term success.

Learning for oneself is one thing but to learn for the organization requires sharing of failed experiences. Unfortunately, as Argyris noted, sharing failures is difficult for individuals to practice within organizations, since most managers like to win and not lose face. Organizational cultures also inhibit sharing failure stories even if they may be more useful than the frequently observed practice of sharing success stories. With success stories, I am never certain of the counter factual. Perhaps another decision may have been even more successful. The organizational or team acceptance to share failures will often be driven by the attitude of the leader. Is it open and developmental or is it judgemental?

Section 7

Managing Finances

Few things cause adults as much stress as grappling with their personal finances. In the West, it is one of the leading causes of divorce. Most people are not experts in finance and find the prospect of managing investments rather daunting. There is an entire industry that exists to reduce the uncertainty faced by consumers and 'help' them. Unfortunately, as has been repeatedly demonstrated, the finance industry exists to help itself, not the investor.

Investors repeatedly make poor decisions with respect to personal finance, many of which could be avoided through education. But too many of us freeze in the face of numbers. Finance seems like learning a foreign language. The three typical mistakes made by people as investors are relatively easily overcome with some self-discipline.

First, waiting too long to start saving and not planning for enough years in retirement. Given the magic of compounding, it is better to start early, even if the amount saved is small. And, many of us, based on the advancement in nutrition and medicine, will live a lot longer than we thought. As a result, retirement savings must go much further.

Second is that even when we do save, we employ the wrong strategies. Instead of trying to pick individual stocks or investing in high-risk categories, boring is better. Investing in low-cost passive funds[1] has been so well and frequently established that it is impossible to refute. There is no need to be clever.

Third, is there is a need to change one's mindset? What leads individuals to attempt foolish strategies such as picking stocks, buying art as investment, or evading taxes? Greed! Therefore, let me end with one of my favourite observations:

> 'Money is a tool to be used, not an end in itself. I have learned that there are only two ways in which money can make you unhappy. First, you spend more than you earn. Second, you compare yourself with others. Unfortunately, people often get caught in one of these two traps, if not both.'

---

1. A passive fund invests to create a portfolio of stocks that mimes the performance of the benchmark index, such as the S & P 500, it has chosen to track. In contrast, active funds have managers who exercise their judgement in picking stocks they believe will outperform the market.

42

Will You Outlive Your Money?

The answer for most people under the age of fifty in the developed world is unfortunately yes. No wonder, half the people in the advanced economies worry about outliving their money. How did we get here?

For much of human history, the concept of retirement did not exist. One hunted or farmed until one was alive. Or, if fortunate enough to be rich, managed the landed assets. Somewhere in the mid-1800s, the concept of retirement age and pensions emerged in USA and Europe. Around 1890, the German government offered to provide pensions for citizens who lived over the age of seventy.

The USA social security, introduced in 1935, set the retirement age at 65. At that time, the life expectancy for American men was 58. Following this, 65 became the default retirement age in many parts of the developed world and for corporations that offered retirement benefits.

Three Challenges to a Financially Secure Retirement

First, advances in medicine and health have led to vast increases in life expectancy. Over the past 150 years, life expectancy has increased by 2-3 years every decade. Today, children born in advanced economies have a greater than 50 per cent chance of living past the age of 100. Even in India, which ranks 166 in the world among countries for life expectancy by one ranking, the life expectancy of a child born today is 69 years in contrast to 41 years in 1960. Large numbers of Indians now live past their 80th birthday. Simply put, the years spent post retirement is much larger than when pension schemes and retirement ages were instituted. If you are below 50 and risk averse, I suggest you plan for retirement funds based on the assumption that you will live to 100.

Second, while the default retirement age is 65, there is considerable variation around this across countries and jobs. In India, the retirement age varies between 56 and 60 years. It is obvious that the younger one retires, the more funds will be needed for the greater number of post-retirement years. Unfortunately, this problem has been exacerbated by longer life expectancy combined with stagnating, and even lowering of, retirement age. While a few countries have increased, or are trying to increase retirement age, it is not a popular decision.

Public sector unions in many countries have guaranteed pensions (called defined benefit) that are also inflation linked. In such circumstances, as is to be expected, unions continuously negotiate for younger retirement age. In France, Greece, Italy, and USA, some fortunate people can retire below the age of 60 with full benefits. This is especially true where retirement is based on the number of years in service. For example, in Turkey, 25 years of service allows retirement for some employees, making it possible to retire in the mid-40s with full pension!

Third, historically, there were more people working than retired on the rolls, and so, in many cases, the benefits for retirees were covered by the contributions of those currently working. This accounting treatment of pensions by governments and public sector institutions failed to create a dedicated pool of money for future retirees from the contributions. Thus, as people live longer post retirement, there is a worsening unfunded pension problem. For example, Chicago has unfunded pension liabilities equivalent to nineteen years of the city's tax revenues! And, the declining yields in recent years have not helped in computing these liabilities. Detroit had to file bankruptcy because of its pension liability, which enabled the city to lower promised pensions.

Private companies across the world realizing that defined benefit schemes are too risky, as yields on assets can change dramatically and retirees can live longer than anticipated, have moved to defined contribution schemes (where the employee's pension is kept in a dedicated account). This has shifted the risk of retirement from companies to individuals. In the face of this new reality, governments, companies and individuals need to readjust strategies to cope with the retirement problem.

No Easy Answers

Some governments are attempting to make unpopular changes. But the retirement age changes are usually too minor with the implementation date too far out. This avoids impacting those currently working and the resulting backlash. Often, the change in retirement age is to 67 or 68, with this coming in force from 2030 or even beyond. This is just not enough to confront the problem.

As retirement becomes less financially viable, people will need to work into their 70s. Substantial numbers of these working retirees will ask for, and may only be able to, work on a part-time basis. They may also desire longer vacations. Designing work to provide the needed flexibility brings challenges for corporations. A single retirement age for all employees may not be sustainable. Yet firms also do not want to be locked into having to prolong retirement for all employees because the capability (relevance and health) to continue the job differs dramatically between older employees of the same age. This will cause greater anxiety and frustration for employees as they approach the retirement years. A system that is flexible, transparent, trusted, and not prone to manipulation, is not easy to design.

As an individual, even if you have a guaranteed pension, as the Detroit case demonstrates, one should make contingency plans. Unfunded pensions are simply unsustainable and the hour of reckoning is coming sooner than we think. It is advisable to have your own retirement plan rather than trust the employer plan. In addition, consider as stated above, assume the 100-year life and significantly lower yields than have been used historically for calculating the needed pension pot.

Finally, beyond saving more, the longer life span means many individuals will need to work post retirement and a greater emphasis on a healthy lifestyle. Working post retirement requires staying relevant to the job market through keeping oneself updated as well as perhaps mid-career retraining for the jobs of the future. Working longer is only possible if one is healthy. It is not about how long one lives but the quality of that life. Increasingly, the distinction is drawn between 'life expectancy' and 'healthy life expectancy'. For India, while the former is 69, the latter is 60. The need to start a fitness regime and adopting good eating habits immediately is also part of the broader retirement savings conceptualization.

43

Beating the Index or Betting Your Retirement?

One of my favourite subjects is the futility of active investing. A 21 March 2016 *Financial Times* report found that 86 per cent of active equity funds in Europe underperformed the benchmark indices over the past decade. This includes 100 per cent of actively managed funds in the Netherlands over the past five years, as well as 95% in Switzerland and 88% in Denmark! Among US active funds, 98.9% over past ten years, 97% of emerging market funds, and 97.8% of global equity funds underperformed. These percentages are calculated after considering the fees. As I often have remarked, one can beat the index over a year, but as the time horizon gets longer and longer, we are left with Warren Buffet. And, who could have predicted Warren Buffet thirty years ago?

The financial industry is truly run for the employees, not the customers. At least US consumers are becoming savvier as in 2015 active funds had a net outflow of billions while passives attracted net inflows of billions. Of course the smart people in the industry keep coming up with new strategies to beat the index. However, since passive funds are so much cheaper to run than active funds, any new strategy must be able to not only beat the index but must also cover the costs of active management.

More recently, the fad had been for 'smart beta' which would beat the index. One example is value investing, believing cheaper stocks do better than more expensive ones. Other strategies include low volatility, hoping that stable stocks perform relatively better; or momentum – expecting winning stocks to continue their winning streak while losing stocks keep falling out of favour. Sometimes, these strategies may work for a short period. But then everyone piles in and returns fall to normal – i.e., cheaper stocks get bid up. Of course, to show superior performance, active managers find the exact time period of 'over-performance' and then advertise it as 'representative' performance.

If active managers, whose job it is to beat the index, are unable to do so, there is little hope that an individual investor can pick stocks. Why do we believe that we would succeed where experts fail? The academic literature in psychology and behavioural finance has explanations for this. The most important is the 'over-confidence bias', which leads us to believe that we are better than average investors, just as most people believe they are smarter than average, and better than average drivers – all statistically impossible.

Besides over-confidence bias, we also suffer from 'loss aversion' bias. Because we hate to acknowledge loss, people sell those stocks that are doing well and retain those that are underwater in the hope they will turn around and revert to the price paid. By selling the winning stocks in their portfolio too quickly, and holding on to their losing stocks for too long, investors end up with a portfolio of 'losers'.

At cocktails, people will often boast of this or that stock on which they made a lot of money. Two things happen here. First, there is no accounting of the baseline – perhaps they would still have been better off placing their money in a passive fund. Second, they only mention the winners, not the losers, as people want to maintain their positive self-image. You observe this in spades in the art world, especially the contemporary art world. Recently, I was with a couple who are among the largest collectors of Chinese art in the world, having dinner on Singapore's waterfront. The husband was telling me how this artist they bought for five thousand dollars now sells for more than a million. Without knowing the details of their art collection, I remarked to them that since they owned more than 5,000 works by Chinese artists, I suspect most of them could not be sold for anything close to what they had paid for them. The wife looked at me and nodded her head. Most contemporary artists ultimately end up on the garbage heap of the forgotten.

And, finally, even if we acknowledge the losers, the 'attribution bias' leads us to argue that this poor outcome was the result of external factors such as a downturn in the market. However, positive outcomes are attributed to the self – my great insight or efforts led to the glorious victory. This is a stable finding – analysis of annual reports of companies, CEO statements on performance, and numerous other applications confirm it.

The India Situation

If you are a long-term investor and can live with the volatility, then equities is the reasonable option. Most business school academics knowing the research in finance tend to invest only in passive funds for their equity exposure. However, for some reason passive funds do not exist in India. We are still waiting for India's Jack Bogle (champion of passive funds and founder of Vanguard, the largest passive player in the world). Instead, I was informed repeatedly after moving to India that most equity managers – numbers such as 80 per cent were being quoted – beat the index against which they are evaluated.

This outperformance seemed surprising to me until I saw the analysis conducted by my ex-colleague, Elroy Dimson, who was professor of finance at London Business School. All the Indian equity managers have to do to consistently beat the index is to buy all the stocks in the index with the exception of the public sector companies (PSU) that are included in the same index. These large government-owned enterprises run by bureaucrats are perennial underperformers on the stock market.

For assessing performance of any mutual fund manager in India, ideally these PSUs should be removed from the index to create the benchmark. But, as one mutual fund manager remarked to me in a private conversation, no one has ever queried on the expense ratio of the fund, and rarely, on the performance against benchmark. Most investors in India simply ask about the absolute return over the past year and over the past three years. In other words, we are betting our retirement savings.

44

Why Does Anyone Invest in Equities?

The separation of control from ownership in publicly listed companies requires effective corporate governance. As investors have limited visibility, it gives rise to the 'agency problem', where managers, as agents, may not run the company in the best interests of the shareholders. In theory, the board of directors are supposed to protect the investors since the management has considerable discretion in running the firm. The board ensures that management does not steal the funds through private planes and plush carpets as well as direct the funds to suboptimal projects from the investors' perspective.

In the USA, with their dispersed shareholding pattern, there is usually no controlling shareholder (the new tech companies like Amazon or Facebook are exceptions). The shareholders are often represented by large mutual fund managers who are supposed to vote on their behalf. The role of the board, with considerable legal liabilities, is to ensure that the investors' rights are protected and the managers are maximizing shareholder value. The corporate governance challenge in the USA is that the large mutual funds are not activist enough, and CEOs, over their tenure, can be pretty savvy in obtaining considerable 'control' over their boards.

The corporate governance challenge in India is different because ownership, as in other emerging markets, is concentrated. More than 75 per cent of the large Indian listed companies are controlled by family businesses. The 'promoter' owns a substantial proportion of the shares and is intimately involved in the management, either directly as CEO or as chairman of the board of directors. Even when there is a professional CEO, as chairman, the promoter has enough visibility of the operations to make the agency problem of management diverting funds from shareholders a minor concern.

Instead, the corporate governance problem in promoter-led companies is protecting the rights of the minority shareholders. With their control over the companies, promoters can divert funds to themselves via various schemes such as tunnelling and/ or pursue personal pet projects that cannot be justified from a maximizing shareholder value perspective.

And, even in the USA courts are hesitant to get involved except in the most egregious cases. The ability for a shareholder to get protection via courts is limited – only recently have class action suits been available to Indian shareholders. Consequently, to date, there is no precedent on this.

Another check on poorly run companies in the USA is the possibility of a hostile takeover. However, hostile takeovers are realistically not possible in India. This leaves the independent directors, theoretically not connected to promoters or executives, as the protectors of minority shareholders. Apart from their directors' remuneration, independent directors in India must not have any pecuniary relationship with the company, its promoters, or associated companies.

Are Independent Directors Independent?

People are not always clear as to the role of the board of directors. The most important role is monitoring for the agency problem, which in India is protecting the minority shareholders from being ripped off by promoters. In practice, boards must also ensure compliance with laws, approve the strategic direction (rather than make strategy), as well as select and motivate the CEO.

One unarticulated role of board members in India is providing resources via their connections. Therefore, boards of companies, especially in industries where the hand of the government looms large (regulated like telecoms or infrastructure related), are heavily populated by ex-bureaucrats who have access to the halls of power. Typically, based on my personal observations, these directors make no substantive contributions during board meetings but are deployed when information or a favour is needed.

On paper, the laws in India are as stringent as anywhere in the world with respect to independent directors. The problem is how it plays out in practice. Increasingly, I have come to believe that an 'independent director' is an oxymoron. Since promoters can vote on the appointment of independent directors, and minority shareholders rarely bother to exercise their voting rights, effectively promoters select the independent directors. Furthermore, the compensation for directors can be different among directors serving on the same board, usually determined at the whim of the promoter. In such a situation, who is going to vote against the promoter?

The Tata saga demonstrated that even someone as powerful as Nusli Wadia was outed for voting against the expressed wishes of the promoter. Most independent directors have much less stature in the absence of their directorships and are definitely not as wealthy. More generally, if an independent director dissents, they get a reputation of being difficult. This will make any further appointments to boards impossible in a country where the social and economic ties between elites are highly intertwined.

Evidence from China

China provides interesting empirical evidence on directors. In 2001, China passed a unique law that required board members of public firms to reveal when they dissent from the majority opinion, along with an explanation for the vote. A fascinating paper demonstrated that dissent by board members is rare.[1] Based on my experience, I am sure if the data for India was available, it would show identical results. I cannot recall the last time a board member dissented on a board I served.

Juan Ma's paper had three other findings which buttress my argument on independent directors being an oxymoron. First, dissent is correlated with breakdown of social ties between the independent director and the board chairperson. Most often, dissent happened after the board chair who appointed the independent director had left the board. Or, in the 60 days prior

1. Juan Ma and Tarun Khanna (2016), 'Independent directors' dissent on boards: Evidence from listed companies in China,' *Strategic Management Journal*, 1547-1557.

to departure of the board chair or departure of the independent director.

Second, dissenting directors were punished. Dissent substantially increased the likelihood of the dissenting director exiting the director labour market. It also resulted in more than 10 per cent estimated loss of annual income. Third, while dissent could be interpreted as a sign of strong corporate governance, firms saw an average share price drop of 0.97 per cent on the days in which the dissent was announced.

The unfortunate message is that if you wish to protect yourself and the stock price of the company, do not dissent. However, I doubt directors anywhere themselves need such advice as they are already aware of it.

Why Does Anybody Invest in Equities?

Given the power of promoters in India, the returns to shareholders are completely at the discretion of the promoter. It is surprising that anybody agrees to provide equity under these circumstances. However, minority shareholders do have soft protection through reputational effects. Many promoters need to, and have returned, to capital markets for future projects and companies. In the absence of fair treatment of minority shareholders, their ability to raise money in capital markets will be severely restricted.

In some sense, minority shareholders rely on the benevolence of promoters. I recall a particularly long annual general meeting (AGM) where the promoter chairman was patiently answering questions from small shareholders long after the allocated time for Q&A. I asked him why he was so patient. His response: I know all these shareholders from past AGMs. They invested in my grandfather and father's companies. They are the first to invest in any company I float. This is their only day in the year with me. Till they have questions, I am happy to be here.

Finally, data from the past twenty years indicates that the risk premium in India for equity holders is 8 per cent per annum. This is relatively large compared to developed markets. Given an economy that is growing fast with considerable future potential as well as the large equity risk premium, minority shareholders may believe that they are being adequately compensated for inadequate corporate governance. Yet, the fact that only 2 per cent of the Indian population participates in equities, and even the rich have large fixed deposits with banks, implies that the arguments above have limited persuasive power.

45

Is Art an Investment?

As an academic, I pay little attention to the spectacular individual success stories of a particular Tyeb Mehta or Souza painting selling for more than a million dollars. Instead, I will reflect on the characteristics of art as an investment vehicle and the empirical evidence comparing long-term financial returns from art versus other asset classes. In addition, as a collector, I will elaborate why anyone would buy art, given its lacklustre financial performance.

Art as Investment

Compared to other asset classes, art suffers from at least five drawbacks as an investment vehicle. If you suddenly need to sell the masterpiece that you happen to own, it will soon become apparent that the art market is not transparent as no two people agree on what the appropriate valuation is. Moreover, it is an illiquid asset. The Indian art market is especially shallow, with relatively few buyers. Furthermore, high transaction costs can eat up as much as 30 per cent (at auctions) compared to selling stocks at a few pennies. And, all of this is before accounting for the fact that unlike property, stocks, and bonds, there is no underlying income stream such as rentals, dividends, or interest received whilst owning the masterpiece. On top of that, the owner usually has to pay for storage and insurance costs.

Several academic studies have been conducted comparing the long-term average financial returns of art versus more traditional investment vehicles.[1] These studies usually compare the performance of an art index with returns from equities and bonds. The studies concentrate on paintings and the period of comparison is at least 25 years, with some studies tracking as much as 300 years of data. There are different ways of constructing the art index but the most popular way is through repeat sales of the same painting at auctions, requiring at least two price observations per painting before it can be included in the database. This means that returns reported for art in these studies are upwardly biased for two reasons. First, the relatively substantial transaction costs are unaccounted for. Second, the method suffers from what is called survivor bias – many of the contemporary artist paintings sold which subsequently become worthless never come up for a repeat sale. In other words, the returns reported for art below are actually a rosier picture than reality.

The real annual returns (subtracting inflation from nominal returns) on paintings reported in the empirical studies range from 0.6 to 5.0, with a median return of 2.6 per cent. Even

---

1. Benjamin R. Mandel (2009), 'Art as an investment and conspicuous consumption good,' *American Economic Review*, 1653-63.

in the Mei and Moses study, which is most popular with art professionals because it shows the highest annual real return to art of 4.9 per cent per annum for the years 1875 to 2000, art fails to outperform equities (S&P 500 or Dow Jones industrial index).[2] Vis-à-vis bonds, the story is slightly more complex but art underperforms corporate bonds and only slightly outperforms the relatively risk-free US government bonds. And, by the way, the results are even worse for masterpieces, going against the conventional industry wisdom that argues for buying the best and most famous works.

Despite the underperformance, it could be argued that art belongs in the investment portfolio if it has lower volatility or is uncorrelated with equities. The news on both these fronts is not encouraging. The volatility of art as measured by the variance of returns is at least twice that of equities or corporate bonds. And, art indices typically have a positive correlation with equities and negative correlations with bonds or treasury bills. In financial theory terms, this means that art is dominated by other asset classes in a portfolio that seeks to maximize returns and minimize variance.

The Collector

Over the years, I have built up a collection of paintings by Jamini Roy (1887-1972), the father of modern Indian art. On his death, deeming them national heritage, the government banned all exports of his paintings. My Jamini collection comprising 60-70 paintings is one of the largest outside of the Indian museums

---

2. Jianping Mei and Michael Moses (2002), 'Art as an investment and the underperformance of masterpieces,' *American Economic Review*, 92(5): 1656–68.

in Calcutta and Delhi. Given that I know the investment performance of art, the obvious question is, why do I collect art?

Four underlying motivations drive the purchase of art:

- First are what I call 'speculators'. They buy art as an investment, and, therefore, rightly diversify the portfolio by buying different artists. However, as explained above, there is considerable misunderstanding regarding art as an investment vehicle.
- Second are people who can be termed as 'decorators'. They buy whatever catches their eye and will gel well with the furnishings in their office or home. The art is a reflection of their taste and their acquisitions tend to be eclectic.
- Third are the 'strivers'. They buy art as status symbols. It helps demonstrate that they have arrived. Typically, their acquisitions are well recognized works so that the viewer immediately knows the value of the work and hence the scale of the owner's success.
- Finally, there are the 'collectors', who are motivated by passion for the art. With no plans to sell the paintings, the market value of the works is irrelevant to them. They get aesthetic pleasure from a painting and from being a custodian of an artist's genius.

Unlike other investment products such as bonds and equities, art is also a consumption product. I do not see art as an investment to fund future consumption. Any money put aside for artworks is after these investment needs have been fulfilled, not in lieu of it. So, readers, think twice when someone sells you art as an investment. Buy it if you like it, but consider, would you still love it if the value halved? And if you are trying to invest in the even more risky contemporary art market solely to make money, consider the casino or buying a lottery ticket.

The Collection

In 2015, the Museo delle Culture in Lugano, Switzerland hosted a three-month exhibition of my collection of Jamini Roys. As those who are in the art world know, single collector museum shows are rare. How does one make a collection?

The big idea in collecting is to limit yourself; only then can your collection become something meaningful. It's the vision behind it that helps make it more than the sum of the parts. This is strategy – it's about making choices in pursuit of a unique position in the industry, not just throwing resources.

A collection of 70 Jaminis is unique in contrast to a collection of 70 paintings by multiple Indian artists, without an overarching theme. For example, a collection of, let's say, a few of Husains, few Razas, few Souzas, and so on is interesting but like so many other Indian art collections. When introducing me in the art world, they say he is the Jamini collector – relevant, differentiated, and credible USP (unique selling proposition) – whereas it is hard to describe immediately what the other collections are, so one can only say that he/she has a great art collection. What I taught, be distinct or be extinct, is what was executed with my art collection.

The Artist

For Jamini, as with any other Indian artist, the challenge is become unique (instantly recognizable) + modern (not about what the eye can see as the camera does that better but what the mind can imagine) + Indian (inspired but not a prisoner). Jamini was the first Indian artist to resolve this. Being a great artist is about having a big unique idea – the USP. Many outstanding painters are therefore not great artists because they lack the 'idea'. For example, in the Bengal school, Abanindranath Tagore and Nandalal Bose come to mind.

Modern art is all about capturing an object, an emotion, an idea with a few strokes. Jamini pushed for simplicity similar to Picasso and other modern masters like Matisse. As de Saint-Exupery said: 'You know you've achieved perfection in design, not when you have nothing more to add, but when you have nothing more to take away.'

I have always believed making things simple is extraordinarily hard, while making them complex is easy. The best teachers make the complex simple. Jamini did the same. For example, he argued that to paint a successful mother, one must capture two attributes – love and strength. It took him decades to get to the six strokes with which to capture a mother (see image).

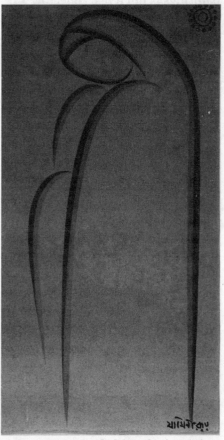

Jamini Roy, untitled (Mother), 1950s

As Einstein noted: 'Everything should be made as simple as possible, but not simpler.' If you take too much out of something then that's simple, but you lose function, as it still must look like a mother.

As art has progressed, a frequent observation is that beautiful art like Jamini is too easy to collect. For example, Lucian Freud remarked: What do I ask of a painting? I ask it to astonish, disturb, seduce, convince. Unlike Freud, Jamini does not disturb, and this is why some may conclude that a collector of Jamini paintings is not a real collector.

46

Why Do People Evade Taxes?

Gary Becker, the Nobel Laureate in economics, developed an elegant model of tax evasion based on economic factors. He contended that tax evasion was determined by the tradeoff between tax rates and the cost of punishment for noncompliance. Higher tax rates increase the incentive to cheat as one saves more money from evasion, while the cost of noncompliance deters avoidance. However, both these factors differ dramatically across countries. For example, in the United States, cheating on taxes is a criminal offence and many famous personalities have been imprisoned as a consequence. In Switzerland, it is a civil offence: they levy a fine, then send you back to work in order to earn and pay.

My argument here is that economic factors are not sufficient to explain tax evasion. Some Scandinavian countries with high tax rates and comfortable prisons have low tax evasion. Something else must be at work. My thesis is that the psychological factor of 'citizen trust' is an important determinant in explaining the pervasiveness of tax evasion in countries such as India.

With respect to taxation, citizens need to sense three types of trust:

1. The taxes levied will be used to pay for valued services.
2. Their fellow citizens will pay their due share.
3. There is a fair process for revenue collection.

The problem in India, where estimates show only 1 per cent of the population pays income tax, is that the trust of citizens on all these three dimensions is low. India compares poorly from this standpoint with the United States, the United Kingdom, Singapore and Switzerland, four other countries that I have lived in.

Providing services that individuals cannot procure for themselves – infrastructure, law and order, and the like – is a fundamental duty of governments. Taxes are necessary for this. While governments will always be inefficient because they are spending someone else's money rather then their own, it is a question of how inefficient they are.

In the Indian context, we see a crisis of trust between citizens and the government. While total revenue collection in the country over the past decade has grown by leaps and bounds, citizens do not see any tangible effects on their lives. For example, roads are worse, public transportation is broken, the police are viewed as widely corrupt, and government schools and hospitals are always the last resort. Consequently, Indians do not see their taxes being used efficiently.

The second dimension of trust is the belief that your fellow citizens will pay their due share. In India, the perception is that the largest tax offenders go scot free, while the more honest or compliant individuals and enterprises are pursued aggressively. To many, it seems there is a penalty for being honest. This is a problem of enforcement.

The third trust factor is about there being a fair process of revenue collection. What I have found in my research is that trust is determined by perceptions of 'outcome fairness' and 'procedural fairness'. More interestingly, my research indicates that outcome fairness (e.g., tax rates) will be less of a determinant of citizens' trust than procedural fairness.[1]

A fair process incorporates six dimensions. To improve these should be the agenda for tax authorities.

1. **Bilateral Communication:** Power over others often means that we listen less to them and our communication becomes one-sided. Two-way communication that engages citizens and allows them to give suggestions and complaints helps build trust.

2. **Impartiality:** This has to do with consistency of policies and their application over time. While everyone cannot be treated identically, the system can be more equitable. A lot of the taxation issues that multinationals are facing in India are linked to this aspect of justice. It is impossible to plan without consistent policies.

3. **Refutability:** The ability to appeal against tax decisions and have them resolved in a fast and cost-efficient manner

---

1. Nirmalya Kumar (1996), 'The power of trust in manufacturer-retailer relationships,' *Harvard Business Review*, November-December, 92-105.

is crucial. This is a huge problem in India, where the legal system is painfully slow in resolving disputes.

4. **Explanation:** That means providing citizens with a coherent rationale for decisions and policies, and it calls for greater transparency. The more power we have, the less we feel the need to explain our decisions. But research indicates that the same decision with an explanation attached is seen as fairer than one without.

5. **Familiarity:** An understanding of the local conditions under which businesses operate is necessary. Think of service tax and the small business unit where both husband and wife work punishing hours. Perhaps they have a turnover of Rs10 million and a profit of Rs 1 million. Now, with the service tax implication, they have to hire a new person and do lots of paperwork. The system must have empathy for such folks, which is why small business owners in countries such as the United States and the United Kingdom are exempted from many regulations and taxes, or have to comply with a simple process that dramatically reduces filing requirements.

6. **Interactional Justice:** You have to treat people with courtesy and respect. For example, in Singapore you can pay customs duty on wine by presenting your credit card and filling out a form on an app. Often, collections increase if the process is easier, faster and respectful. Not only that, the bureaucrat in the tax office in Singapore addresses you, the citizen, as 'Sir'!

These six principles are the levers to help improve the citizen's trust in the tax system. Public trust is one of the most precious assets that a country can have. It is the cornerstone of effective governance, the main ingredient to promote economic growth and social progress.

As Ralph Waldo Emerson said, 'Our distrust is very expensive.'

Section 8

Managing Life

My life has been devoted to learning. How does one learn? And, how does one learn about life? For me, this takes place through the power of observation, the power of experience, and the power of reflection.

Observation of others and reading voraciously were my first teachers. There are always others who know more about specific subjects. Whether it is drinking wine, listening to music, appreciating art, or investing in the stock market, I will first turn to learning from the experts. To do something 'just for fun' is no fun for me. I must immerse myself in an activity and turn it into a learning expedition. As Bertrand Russell said, 'to be able to fill leisure intelligently is the last product of civilization'.

The power of experience is how most of us learn. But all experiences are not equal. Those that had the greatest potential for learning for me were the ones when I struggled the most to master an unfamiliar environment. Clearly, the doctoral programme at Northwestern University, the faculty position at IMD when I was suddenly thrust into executive education, and the relatively short tenure as an executive at Tata were the most valuable for the steep change they made in my personal development.

But observation and experience are only valuable when combined with reflection. Two people observing the same thing or experiencing the same incident will take away vastly different learnings because of the reflection and dedication that they bring to it. There are no shortcuts on the long walk to excellence. One never stops learning, because life never stops teaching. We all are work in progress.

47

Is Everyone Trying to Be Someone They Are Not?

Of course, any question that begins with 'everyone' must be false. But, I often deliberately espouse provocative positions for three reasons. First, it helps unfreeze others as they feel compelled to stake an opposing view and start a conversation. Second, their counter arguments help me refine and improve my own arguments by seeking the limits of the position I have adopted. Finally, I am a bit of a rabble-rouser, and so I take some delight in stirring up the pot.

Stretching Oneself

Most of us are trying to become better as human beings and at what we do. This must be encouraged. As I will note in the next chapter, 'Does IQ Matter?', to become skilled at anything requires extraordinary effort. Similarly, to improve as human beings, we try to hone our strengths and work on our weaknesses. This is also praiseworthy.

Personally, I have always concentrated on improving my strengths instead of overcoming my weaknesses. The logic being that even after enormous effort, the chances are that I will be, at best, average on my weaker attributes. In contrast, by working on my strengths, I aspire to be an outlier on those. Consistent with my contention in chapters 19 (Does Anybody Hate You?) and 45 (Is Art an Investment?):

Either you are distinct, or you are extinct.

People buy something despite its weaknesses because it is occupying a corner solution (in a multidimensional attribute model). In this view, one accepts reducing some of the negative attributes only to a level that it does not deter too many buyers. The cost of this strategy of focusing on strengths and living with the weaknesses is a smaller target market. But then, how much applause does one need?

What I am referring to when observing that 'everyone is trying to be someone they are not' is situations in which one fails the authenticity test. When our family, friends, and even society push us to be something that we are not, and cannot pull off, we must resist.

It is surprising how many of us waste so much of our lives trying to display qualities we do not possess and gain applause we cannot hold. As we become older, we hope to get more comfortable in our own skin. When you do not need adulation any more, you are finally free to be yourself. As the Greek poet, Horace, observed two thousand years ago:

Life is about coming back to yourself as a friend.

Positive Illusions

The above discussion allows me to introduce the concept of positive illusions. Traditionally, in psychology, having inaccurate positive beliefs about oneself was seen as dysfunctional to emotional well-being. One would perhaps label such persons as delusional. Consequently, accurate perceptions of oneself was considered an essential element of mental health.

Then came the fascinating research by Shelley Taylor which established that most people have 'positive illusions' about themselves.[1] Specifically, her research demonstrated that people suffer from positive illusions in three important spheres:

1. Viewing ourselves in unrealistically positive terms.
2. Believing we have greater control over the environment than is the case.
3. Holding assessments of the future that are more optimistic than base-rate data can justify.

Given the prevalence of these beliefs, and that, by definition, it is not tenable to classify the majority as abnormal, one must conclude that accurate perceptions are not essential for mental

---

1. See Shelley E. Taylor (1989), *Positive Illusions: Creative Self-deception and the Healthy Mind* (Basic Books).

health. And, people are quite ingenious in maintaining such inflated self-perceptions through strategies such as:

1. Choosing attributes for comparisons with others on which you are advantaged.
2. Defining attributes in ways that reflect on your perceived strengths.
3. Selecting comparison groups that are worse so as to guarantee favourable self-perceptions.

In fact, some researchers find that accurate and balanced perceptions of oneself, which traditionally was thought to be associated with a well-adjusted individual, to be correlated with depression. Others argue, however, that depression is more typically related to negatively biased perceptions rather than accurate perceptions. Regardless, that the term depressive realism is often used in this situation is revealing.

Since Shelley Taylor's paper, many benefits of these optimistic self-beliefs, sometimes also measured as self-efficacy, have been established. For young children, it helps acquire language skills, develop motor skills, and aids problem solving. In adults, positive illusions help produce more creative work, lead to greater success, aid positive social relationships as well as lead to a greater ability to deal with stressful situations such as coping with severe health problems.

Dilemma

Clearly, we need to consider ourselves greater than we are if we are to accomplish anything worthwhile and overcome the obstacles to ambitious goals. If we only followed accurate self-beliefs, we would never attempt things that are outside our current capabilities, require extraordinary effort, and at which there is a chance of failing (see chapter 41, Must you fail to learn?). However, it is only through such experiences that we grow and achieve our fullest potential.

On the other hand, these positive illusions at the extreme can be so self-aggrandizing that one loses touch with reality. It can lead us to compete against those whom we have no chance of beating. Unfortunately, I have often observed the dysfunctional effects of this situation in the workplace. The results are entirely predictable with the delusional person ultimately feeling frustrated, and sometimes, depressed. So therein lies the dilemma. We need positive illusions, but within reason.

48

Does IQ Matter?

After settling into the Tata group, I became concerned that we were hiring too many people with a similar profile. To trigger this conversation, I included an abbreviated intelligence (IQ) test available on the internet to the readers of my weekend email.

Some of my Tata colleagues sent their individual scores to me. Among those who responded, scores of 156, 145, 134, and 100 were obtained by 4, 7, 7, and 1 person respectively. Given that the IQ test has a mean of 100 with a standard deviation of 15, this was impressive. No one came close to my low score of 78. Admittedly, this was not a representative sample, but it was adequate to raise the question: does IQ matter?

The problem with IQ tests is that they confuse being smart with one type of intelligence; they assume that intelligence is a fixed trait and ignore other factors that determine success. There is a lot of research on, and intuitively we understand, that intelligent people may not be successful as they may not put in the effort or lack emotional intelligence. We also understand that people scoring low on these tests can still be successful as intelligence is not the only determinant of success.

My score is more unusual because despite the low score, I have performed well in academic examinations. Robert Sternberg is perhaps the leading psychologist in this area. He had a low IQ score but demonstrated, with practice, he could increase his score. I suspect this may be true for me.

The more important issue is that we often see people perform on a single task or test, and ascribe general levels of intelligence or smarts to them. All performance on a task tells us is the person's skill to do that task at that particular moment. Yes, general intelligence matters, as does aptitude, but how well one does on a particular task is determined largely by the strategy adopted (clear goals, smart strategy, learning orientation) and the effort (persistence) expended. We tend to overlook these last two factors.

Carol Dweck

Carol Dweck demonstrated that people either hold the belief that intelligence is a fixed trait or that it is a malleable trait.

Those believing intelligence is 'fixed' agree:

- A person has a certain finite amount which is resistant to change.
- Some people are lucky and have it, whilst others are not so fortunate.
- Most people with this belief also believe that they have it and rank amongst the intelligent.

In contrast, those believing intelligence is a 'malleable' trait report:

- Intelligence is a potential that can be developed over time.
- It is not that everybody is the same, but emphasize the idea that everyone can become smarter by developing their potential.
- It is not about whether you are ranked among the intellectual elite but about working hard, taking challenges, striving to learn and grow intellectually.

My favourite study is Mueller & Dweck (1998), where they:[1]

- Randomly assigned children to two groups and gave them all a puzzle that was age appropriate. Most of them solved it, and the average performance of the two groups was similar.
- After their performance, one of the groups was praised for their 'intelligence', while the other group was praised for the 'effort' that they had put into solving the puzzle.
- Then both groups were asked if they would like a similar puzzle or a harder one. In the 'intelligence' feedback group, most chose the safer task (easier puzzle) while 90 per cent chose the more challenging puzzle in the 'effort' group. In other words, the 'intelligent' group had become so invested in looking smart that they gave up the opportunity to learn and become smarter.
- Everyone was given the harder puzzle to solve.

---

1. Claudia M. Mueller and Carol S. Dweck (1998), 'Praise for intelligence can undermine children's motivation and performance,' *Journal of Personality and Social Psychology*, 75, 1, 33-52.

- The intelligence group quickly gave up and demonstrated a decline in enjoyment in the task. When the allotted time was over, they immediately returned the puzzle. They now held beliefs that they were not smart and not good at the task.
- The 'effort' group persisted and at the end of the allocated time asked for more time. If success taught them that they had put in the effort, then failure implied greater effort was necessary. They did not doubt their intelligence, simply that the task called for more effort. Interestingly, some of these students requested the name of the puzzle so they could ask their parents to buy it and continue trying it at home.
- Both groups were then assigned a third task, equal in difficulty to the first. The intelligence group demonstrated a decline in performance. Perhaps they gave up. In contrast, the effort group increased performance as they were inspired by the setback. In other words, the simple manipulation of feedback led to a difference in their subsequent performance between the two groups, where none existed at the start (between tasks 1 and 3 of equal difficulty).
- When asked to report their performance to a friend who was not in the room, 40 per cent in the 'intelligence' group lied about their performance, compared to few in the 'effort' group.

The conclusion from this study was that we are making people dumb by telling them they are smart. It is a significant study that implies that by praising our children/employees that they are intelligent when they succeed on a task, we are consigning them to mediocrity. It is much more useful to tell them when they succeed that it is the result of their strategy or effort. This allows them to attribute failure on a task to the strategy employed or their effort, both of which can be varied.

Blessed with Low IQ

Dweck's research has been significant in my life. Nobody ever thought I was particularly intelligent (excluding my mother) until 1997/98, when I started noticing that executives after a classroom session or consulting assignment would tell me that I was the most intelligent person they had met. But what they had just seen was a demonstration of a skill I had honed over a decade by that time. The results simply reflected my performance on the task at that moment. More broadly, this performance:

- Probably reflected my actual skill at that time.
- Had less to do with my broader intelligence.
- Even less to do with intellectual potential or ability to expand skills.
- Little to do with my self-worth as a person.

To compensate for my low IQ score, I would reach work at 6:00 am. This meant leaving home at 5:45 in Switzerland and 5:15 in UK/USA. As the average colleague appeared around 8:30, I had more than a two-hour advantage. To compensate for that much additional effort is difficult, provided I was following the right strategy (otherwise the effort is just wasted). This is why my advice to my daughter is: give them intelligence, you take effort and strategy. Only on my 50th birthday, having achieved all my career goals, I decided enough is enough, and to finally enjoy breakfast at home.

Is Working Hard for the Untalented?

Unfortunately, people deny the power of effort. Popular culture holds the myth that effort is only for the incompetent. This leads to:

- The belief that things come easily to geniuses. But, even geniuses work extraordinarily hard to make great discoveries.
- While it is true that if two people do the exact same task, one will require less effort, all it implies is the person is more skilled at doing that task at that point of time.
- When confronted with a difficult task requiring a lot of effort, those who hold intelligence as fixed worry about their intelligence and get distracted by concerns of inadequacy.
- Self-handicapping occurs by those who hold intelligence as fixed by trying to act like they do not need to put in a lot of effort, when effort is most needed.

So, let me conclude with a quote from the late American President, Calvin Coolidge: 'Nothing in the world can take the place of persistence. Talent will not; nothing is more common than unsuccessful men with talent. Genius will not; unrewarded genius is almost a proverb. Education will not; the world is full of educated derelicts. Persistence and determination alone are omnipotent.'

49

Is Management a Noble Profession?

One consequence of the 2008 financial crisis, the deleterious impact of which still persists on employment and income, is that it tarnished the image of bankers and managers. Despite some of them believing that they are 'doing God's work', I would be hard pressed to defend bankers. Yet, even before the financial crisis, business executives were not particularly admired or appreciated by the masses.

At the risk of eliciting laughter, I believe that there is fundamental lack of understanding of why management is necessary, and consequently, why management is a noble profession. I realize it is relatively easy to make fun of the many unnecessary bureaucratic procedures that we all face every day in our encounters with the government, as well as the practices of profiteering businesses. But, this should not take away from the critical role of managers in any society, regardless of whether they serve in the non-profit or profit sectors.

Managers are indispensable because no society, no matter how rich, has the resources to fulfil all the aspirations of its inhabitants. There has to be some form of rationing. This can be done by rules, as government agencies and non-profits do, based one hopes on 'need'. Alternatively, it can be via the price mechanism (can you afford it?) as businesses and markets do. Neither mechanism is perfect.

The drawbacks of each can be observed clearly by contrasting the challenges of the UK Health Care System (NHS) with those of the USA. UK, which relies on need, has long waiting times, while the USA, which relies on markets, has many uninsured. There is rationing of health care in both systems. Of course, it is more obvious in the UK's NHS since everybody is eligible for care. If someone does not receive care in UK, the blame falls on the government as healthcare is viewed as a right.

In contrast, in the USA's private system, the 'blame' or 'responsibility' of rationing health care is transferred to the individual rather than the government as it is the individual's responsibility to buy adequate insurance. In general, the masses, despite misgivings, will be more satisfied in the UK system, while the elites will be happier in the US system.

Returning to my thesis, the point I am trying to drive towards is that great managers in either system, through efficient operations, manage to serve more people (citizens or customers) at lower costs. Efficiency (input/output ratios) is the magic potion that should be the focus of managers, regardless of whether they are driven by the altruistic or the profit motive. And, for the cynical, even in the profit-driven business world, thoughtful entrepreneurs and managers realize that it is only by serving many customers efficiently that one creates the most wealth for one's business[1] and oneself.

Low Cost Business Model

The low cost business model employed by companies like Aravind Eye Hospital, EasyJet, IKEA, Vanguard, and Walmart is especially illustrative of how management, through more efficient use of resources, can help increase living standards.

Take the case of Aldi from Germany, often referred to as a hard-discount store. It is a minimally decorated outlet that sells a small assortment of foodstuffs and household goods – typically 1,000 items (SKUs) compared to a usual supermarket that stocks 30,000 SKUs.[2] They are small retail stores with comparably lower staffing levels, and typically located in low-rent districts. Hard discounters have an extremely efficient supply chain, thanks largely to their limited SKU numbers and private-label focus, which make for a simpler operation. Aldi's costs add 13 per cent or 14 per cent to the procurement price – 2 per cent each for logistics, rental, overhead, and marketing, plus about 5 per cent for staff. Its efficiency allows Aldi to offer products at startlingly low prices.

By keeping SKU numbers low, Aldi can cut supply chain costs because their own brands account for 80 per cent of the SKUs. Since these private labels are typically priced at 50 per cent below manufacturers' brands, their success has helped rich and poor consumers cover their essential needs at much lower costs. And, yes, it has resulted in competitive pressures for the bloated traditional supermarkets and brand manufacturers.

---

1. Nirmalya Kumar (2006), 'Strategies to fight low cost strategies,' *Harvard Business Review*, 84 (December) 104-12.
2. Nirmalya Kumar and Jan Benedict Steenkamp (2009), 'Don't be undersold!' *Harvard Business Review*, December, 90-95.

Even if a company does not adopt the low-cost model, unless one is into luxury brands (where higher price is part of the customer proposition), all managers should be seeking greater efficiency (obtaining more output with fewer resources). Some of these gains can be directed to increasing profitability, but the rest should be devoted to reducing prices and / or investing in innovation. This helps expand the market (by lowering / maintaining prices), offer better products over time (through innovation), and build more sustainable organizations (through profitability).

Bureaucratic Encounters

Management can help improve lives because ultimately most of our interactions are with organizations, from the daily Starbucks to the infrequent immigration service. Countries that are developed have more efficient processes, designed by better managers. Unfortunately, often, especially in less developed markets, the belief is that it is scarce resource endowments that is the reason for difference with developed world.

Consider a visit to Switzerland. At the immigration desk, the encounter takes less than 30 seconds and there is no immigration form to complete. In fact, with the obvious exception of USA, the shorter the immigration form for tourists, the more developed the country is. Resources, time and money, are not wasted on inefficient processes. And, this is despite more people wanting to immigrate to Switzerland than India.

Similarly, previously I was attempting to keep my mobile numbers with Vodafone India and Vodafone UK by just changing the billing to my personal account instead of being billed to my former employer. It was not easy in either country. Yet, the UK process was completed with fewer forms and interactions. For India, despite providing voluminous back-up documents, I am still waiting, after two unsuccessful phone calls. Again, resources of both Vodafone and my time are limited. Management, via bureaucratic processes and through efficient utilization, makes large differences between societies.

Take a Bow

So, managers all over the world, especially in the business world, do not be shy. Take a bow for the valuable work that you do. And remember, the challenge is to serve ever greater numbers of satisfied customers through higher efficiency, while generating profits for the company.

50

Are You Getting Enough Sleep?

It is always interesting to hear people at work boasting about how little sleep they got the night before. At times, I too confess to being guilty on this count. It appears almost to be a badge of honour among top executives to say, 'I slept only four hours last night and, look at me, I'm at work this morning.'

Donald Trump repeatedly bragged about not needing much sleep while needling his opponents for being low energy and lacking stamina. Margaret Thatcher and Bill Clinton are often evoked as successful people who reportedly slept only four hours a night on a regular basis. Sam Walton, the founder of Walmart, got to work at 4 am every day. This made me feel ashamed that I used to arrive only by 6 am at Harvard, IMD and London Business School, all places where I knew the cleaning staff on a first-name basis.

Given that we would send a truck driver home if we knew he or she had had just four hours of sleep the previous night, I am surprised we do not tell top executives the same. While they may not be operating a heavy vehicle that can crash, fatigue lowers responsiveness, and the decisions that managers make can affect thousands of lives.

Research has documented that sleeplessness leads to slower mental functioning. The lack of sleep makes it harder for an individual to sustain attention and maintain peak cognitive performance. Studies demonstrate that sleeplessness lengthens response time, impedes judgement and interferes with effective problem solving. And, over the long term, lack of sleep is associated with all types of maladies, from high blood pressure to obesity.

Why Do We Need Sleep

There is interesting research on the need for sleep. If we go back to our hunter-gatherer days, we were most vulnerable to being attacked when asleep. Even when aroused from sleep to danger, our reaction time is slow since our muscles are muted from inactivity. Consequently, sleep must have some overwhelming functional benefits for us to have put ourselves in such danger. Not only humans, but all animals sleep.

There are several streams of research that reveal the psychological and physiological benefits of sleep. Simply put, it is overnight therapy. Psychologically, through sleep we process memory in a way that helps recalibrate our emotional self. Experiments show that during sleep, we separate significant experiences from the emotional baggage associated with them. This allows us to recall these experiences, and their information-rich content, without the associated emotion (especially pain).

Physiological research shows that during sleep the body recharges itself physically, with the brain and body engaging in important repair functions. Brain scans indicate that during sleep the brain flushes unnecessary matter and fixes systems that are put under stress during the waking hours.

Sleep therapists recommend getting eight hours of sleep a night. However, as both parents are increasingly employed outside the home, and the household chores still have to be done within the same 24 hours a day that are available, lack of sleep is becoming a societal problem. Companies and managers are not helping by pushing for long hours at the workplace.

Wakeful Empathy

On joining the Tata group, I queried one of our smart young executives on the official working hours. She quipped: 10 minutes before your boss comes in and until 10 minutes after their departure. This made me careful about leaving work at a reasonable hour because of the knock-on effects on my team. Those reporting to me would not usually depart until I did.

Unfortunately, top executives often do not realize that the commute of those lower down the food chain is usually longer and they have less help available at home. Furthermore, nowadays the bane of being always connected is that, at least from my own experience, one ends up spending on average an hour a day on work emails between leaving and returning to the office.

All of this means that if you as a top executive are pushing people to work late hours, they are physically unable to have their eight hours of sleep. Without sleep, productivity suffers, creative thinking declines and overall irritability increases – across the organization.

In conclusion, let us stop boasting about how late we stayed in the office. It does nobody any good. There is no need to show how important we are by the number of hours we work. Instead, why not use the time in the office efficiently, delegate more, and have some wakeful empathy for those working under us.

51

Does Parenting Matter?

Sixteen years ago, with the arrival of Maya, I became a father. As all parents feel, it was a transformational event. Sometimes, as new parents, we forget that becoming a parent is something that has happened billions of times before. Yes, it is a unique event, but only for us as individuals, not for humanity.

Given my learning orientation as a good academic, I started by spending a couple of days reading the social science research on children and parenting. The idea was to gain whatever insights I could on this subject as I did not think my parents were a good role model on this front. Much of this research is focused on twins to be able to tease out the effects of genetics on one hand, in contrast to similarities versus differences in the environment (e.g., parenting styles, friends, peers, schools).

The, admittedly, quick scan of the research led me to the conclusion that 'parents matter, parenting does not'. Basically, the research says that 50 per cent of the variance is explained by the genes handed down by the parents, but 'parenting' has failed to show any consistent effects on the future well-being (usually measured as economic success and social success in terms of maintaining relationships) of children. If you are sceptical of this research, just reflect on the siblings in your family. Despite shared genes and parenting, they are so different.

The remaining 50 per cent of the variance is impacted by the environment. The research distinguishes between shared and non-shared environment. Shared environment is what siblings all experience, while non-shared environment captures the unique experiences of siblings raised together. Only non-shared environment has been consistently demonstrated to have an impact.

The most critical non-shared environment is, however, impacted by two choices of the parents – the neighbourhood they live in and the schools they send their children to. Why? Because after genetics, the strongest correlate is the child's best friends or peers, and these are influenced by neighbourhood and school that the child finds themselves in. As a result, non-biological-related adopted children brought up in the same household by the same parents have been shown to turn out to be completely different to each other (as they do not even share genetics).

Smug with this knowledge, when Maya was perhaps two, at a dinner with some friends and Maya's mother, the discussion turned to parenting and children. I pronounced my conclusion – parents matter, parenting does not. I can still see the furious look on the face of Maya's mother, who was spending all her time trying to bring up the kid. She retorted: 'What do I care about the academic research!' Sad to say, my zero EQ has remained an enduring trait. Or, as a dear friend once summarized, so much knowledge, so little wisdom.

How Do You Judge a Good Parent?

In everything I have pursued, my preference is to have an objective criterion (measurable data which is relatively immune to personal control/manipulation). Soon after my daughter's arrival, at lunch with my faculty colleagues at IMD, I asked them, 'How would you know if you are a successful parent?' The goal was to use this group of very smart people to solve the problem of the criterion. I felt they must have reflected on this as parents.

The responses were rather unsatisfactory for the purposes of seeking an objective criterion. Most could not articulate a crisp answer. Perhaps, the best or most frequent one was, 'a happy, well-adjusted child'. Anyway, finding this too vague for my own preferences, I decided the criterion should be: At the age of 25, Maya comes and tells me Dad I hope one day I will be as good a parent as you were. Perhaps, set up for failure. But, then knowing myself, I wouldn't have it any other way.

Conclusion

A couple of years ago, Maya and I were with my mother for our annual vacation with her. My mother is a lady whose IQ is very high but an EQ even lower than mine, if that is possible. The conversation with my mother turns to Maya:

Mom: Maya is growing up very well.
Me: Let's hope so, but she can do much better.
Mom: You really are an incredible dad.

Me: Hmmm don't know, couldn't have learnt that from dad or you.

Mom: Nope.

So, the research is very clear, in fact considered 'laws' in the field of behavioural genetics. As parents, beyond the genes, we bear zero responsibility for impacting the intelligence or personality of our children. But, the fact that we believe we have an influence with our parenting styles does lead us to aspire to be better parents. And, that cannot be a trivial result. Furthermore, despite the research, which progresses by negating findings from the past, it may still be possible that we do sculpt our children after all.

52

Must We Thank Our Stars?

In a 2012 speech at Princeton, the author Michael Lewis summarized my feelings better than I could:

> 'Don't be deceived by life's outcomes. Life's outcomes, while not entirely random, have a huge amount of luck baked into them. Above all, recognize that if you have had success, you have also had luck – and with luck comes obligation. You owe a debt, and not just to your gods. You owe a debt to the unlucky.'

At the age of 23, I recall asking my father for a one-way ticket to the USA and 400 dollars. He had the 400 dollars, but it needed a loan from his friend, which I later repaid, to buy my ticket. What I have learnt observing people who have had successful lives is that it often makes them lose empathy for those less fortunate. It is easy to be seduced by the narrative that 'I did it all on my own.' Using my life as an example, I wish to argue that we are where we are because of others and good old luck.

On applying for an MBA to a dozen schools in USA, only one, University of Illinois at Chicago, exhibited any interest. I appeared on their campus seeking a place to stay. A post on the campus wall led to a meeting with a lady who was offering free lodging if I agreed to babysit her twins every evening. I could not believe my windfall.

Not entirely convinced of my abilities, the university offered only provisional admission for a single quarter. In a lucky break, the first course was marketing taught by the late Professor Chem Narayana, who also happened to be the chair of the department. After observing my performance on the midterm exams, he persuaded the university to give me a scholarship. Not only was my tuition waived, but I also received 6,000 dollars annually tax free for expenses. Suddenly, I was rich, making more money than my father, and living on my own. I never forget that at critical junctures, others have made indispensable and altruistic contributions to move me forward.

In any case, I did not start from nothing. I was privileged to have inherited the right cocktail of genes from my parents: the brain from my mother combined with the physical energy of my father. Reverse this, with no disrespect to my parents, especially my deceased father, it would probably have been a disaster.

I don't know what led my parents to send me to La Martiniere Calcutta. Even today, it is ranked among the top five schools in India and nearly impossible to gain admission into. At the age of seven, I failed the entrance examination. Once again, by chance, my father happened to know a bureaucrat in the education ministry who 'managed' my entry. The students at La Martiniere were drawn from the cream of Calcutta society. It was encounters with them that raised my ambitions and life chances (see chapter 51: Does Parenting Matter?).

Of course, one may retort that any success is explained by my hard work, curiosity, and learning orientation. However, if you think deeply about this, it is not clear that this should be attributed to me. Why do I work hard and aspire for nothing less than perfection? The answer is I can't be otherwise – it's a providential gift of personality, like my many flaws.

Just as in our strengths lie our weaknesses (e.g., confidence can be viewed as arrogance), our flaws can be a source of energy. My irritability comes from the insatiable curiosity, which drives impatience towards anything that is boring, repetitive, and mediocre. Salman Rushdie encapsulated this beautifully as 'the power of negative influences'.

The Outsider

Ever since I can recall, I have been an outsider. Someone who never really fit into any of the worlds I inhabited – family, school, neighbourhood, academic conferences, or workplace. It is hard being an outsider. But it gave me freedom and sharpened my perceptions. Even now, you may see me at a party that I have been forced to attend standing all by myself watching the room.

Once you are not seeking the approval of others, you can strike an independent path. For example, after graduating from the doctoral programme and having started my first academic position, a faculty colleague put me down by saying 'we are academics, but you are an MBA type'. Among academics, this is the worst of all abuses. Realizing that academics would not accept me as one of their own, I learnt to accept not being accepted. My natural obstreperousness now needed no filter.

In the corporate world, I was an academic, and in the academic world, I was a corporate consultant. Similarly, I was viewed as an Indian when outside India, and seen as a foreigner when in India. Once again, it allowed me to be both critical of India as well as critical of those who did not acknowledge the rise of India. I have always believed that one of the primary responsibilities of any academic is to dissent from conventional wisdom as well as the prevailing consensus of their own community. It's not necessary to be an academic to be critical of other academics, but being one helps. Similarly, being from India and a foreigner gave me both insight and independence. Living on the edge of two worlds is where I naturally find my home.

I know how big a deal it is to have been a 'guru' and at schools like Harvard Business School, IMD, and London Business School, as well as the head of strategy for the Tata group or the custodian of a unique heritage art collection. But, I never really saw myself as being part of these worlds. Instead, to me they were colossal cathedrals, demanding homage, while I was the mischievous kid peeking to see what is inside. Finding these worlds rather hypocritical and pompous, I enjoyed being a tease, knowing it annoyed them. Those who have attended my classroom, or have been with me in faculty retreats, corporate meetings at Tata, and at art events will attest this court jester-like ability to speak freely, to reflect on the absurd, the reverse of received wisdom, the overlooked, is what makes for a unique experience.

The talented blues singer Larry Johnson, who was unfortunate to have never found the fame he deserved, once reflected: 'If you are working on a style, little by little competition don't mean nothing because you in your own vein. The next guy do what he do and you do what you do.'[1] My style is my signature.

I have been blessed to have had a life from which I never needed a vacation. Not many people have the luxury of, whenever it ultimately happens, dying with memories, and not with dreams.

Conclusion

We often ascribe our success to our own abilities and hard work, while our failures are attributed to bad luck and unfortunate circumstances. But, if we accept success is largely determined by luck and propitious situations, then empathy for those who have been less fortunate is inevitable. Research demonstrates that such an attitude makes people more open to societal welfare schemes that aim to reduce poverty and equalize life chances. By thinking differently, we can change the world.

---

1. Larry Johnson in the movie *Lightning in a Bottle*, 2005.

About the Author

Nirmalya Kumar is Lee Kong Chian Professor of Marketing at Singapore Management University and Distinguished Academic Fellow at INSEAD Emerging Markets Institute. Previously, he was Member, Group Executive Council at Tata Sons. At Tata Sons, he was responsible for strategy of the $100 billion-plus group with 675,000 employees worldwide, and reported to the chairman, Cyrus Mistry.

As an academic, he has also taught at Columbia University, Harvard Business School, IMD (Switzerland), London Business School, and Northwestern University (Kellogg School of Management). Nirmalya has written seven books, five of which have been published by Harvard Business Press.

Nirmalya is widely published in academic journals such as *Academy of Management Journal, Journal of Marketing,* and the *Journal of Marketing Research.* In addition, he has nine appearances in the *Harvard Business Review.* His publications have attracted more than 19,000 citations on Google Scholar.

As a consultant, coach, and conference speaker, Nirmalya has worked with over fifty Fortune 500 companies in sixty different countries. He has served on several boards of directors including ACC, Ambuja Cement, Bata India, Tata Capital, Tata Chemicals, Ultratech, and Zensar, all with billion dollars plus in capitalization.

Nirmalya received his B.Com. from Calcutta University (graduating first in his class of 5,251 students), his MBA from the University of Illinois at Chicago, and his PhD in marketing from Kellogg Graduate School of Management (winning the Marketing Science Institute's Alden G. Clayton Award for his PhD dissertation).

His work has led to more than a thousand press appearances, six case adoption awards by The Case Centre, as well as several teaching, research, and lifetime achievement honours. In 2010, Speaking.com voted Nirmalya amongst the top five marketing speakers worldwide; the *Economic Times* placed him sixth on the list of Global Indian Thought Leaders; whilst the *Economist* referred to him as a 'rising superstar' in their cover story 'The New Masters of Management'.

He is regularly included in lists such as 50 Best B-School professors in the world, 50 most influential Business School professors, and Thinkers50 (the biannual listing of the top 50 management thinkers in the world). In 2011, he received the Thinkers50 'Global Village Award' for the academic who contributed most to the business community's understanding of globalization and the new frontiers established by the emerging markets.

In his personal life, Nirmalya is a passionate supporter of the arts. He is the custodian of amongst the largest-known private collection of paintings by Jamini Roy (1887-1972; the father of Indian modern art). He has served on the South Asian Acquisition Committee of Tate Modern and been a patron of British Museum. In recognition of his patronage and promotion of South Asian Art, the School of Oriental and African Studies (SOAS), University of London, awarded him an Honorary Fellowship in 2012.

Readers can follow him on LinkedIn and Twitter (@ProfKumar).